EIRIK
(Elementals CT MC)

ALEXI FERREIRA

Copyright © 2021 Alexi Ferreira

All rights reserved.

ISBN: 9798451681701

Love is sometimes hidden within the mist, hard to find but worth the wait.

- Alexi Ferreira

EIRIK 1	3
SIENA 2	15
EIRIK 3	26
SIENA 4	37
EIRIK 5	48
SIENA 6	64
EIRIK 7	75
SIENA 8	87
EIRIK 9	100
SIENA 10	115
EIRIK 11	125
SIENA 12	139
EIRIK 13	152
SIENA 14	170
EIRIK 15	183
SIENA 16	198
EIRIK 17	213
SIENA 18	224
EIRIK 19	235
A MESSAGE FROM ALEXI FERREIRA	245

ACKNOWLEDGMENTS

To my son and daughter that are always there for me, believing in me. To all my readers for all their support, without all of you this dream wouldn't be possible, to my graphic designer JessFX for the great book covers and all your patience with me.

Thank you to all my ladies in A's Guardians you are my encouragement, a special thank you to Tiffany Mann, Kim Butler, Amanda McCurdy, Johanna Matthews and Mandy New. I am very blessed to have such wonderful ladies in my team, and to my wonderful PA's Sydnee Walsh and Mikki Thomas that keep me grounded and on schedule.

EIRIK 1

I lean my head back against the tombstone and close my eyes. It has been a long couple of months, with constant fighting among the Elementals and the Cape Town gangs. Ever since the death of Sean, the Desperados' leader, we have had a constant fight on our hands. When Dag killed Sean, we thought that it would have stopped the war between the Elementals and Desperados, but instead, it has brought more upheaval to us, as two more gangs are upset for losing out on the business they had going with Sean in the trafficking of women.

"I'm tired, Isabela," I murmur softly to not disturb the peacefulness of this place. I've gotten into the habit over the years of coming to Isabela's resting place to talk to her when I'm restless. I smile when I think of the beautiful woman she was, of the joy and laughter that she brought to my life. I knew that she wasn't my mate. I knew that it was impossible for the two of us, but I never dreamed that I would have such little time with her. I always felt guilty in a way for not being able to give her what she most wanted, what in a way she deserved.

When she fell ill, I tried everything to keep her with me for longer, but nothing worked, and she eventually submitted to her illness. How was she not my mate? Still today I am baffled, because in my own way, I loved Isabela, but fate didn't warrant that we be happy. I don't want a mate; I don't believe that I can give a woman what I couldn't give to Isabela. Isabela knew everything about me, and even though I couldn't make her my true mate, I married her and made her my wife to show her that I loved her, that no matter what fate dictated I considered her mine.

Her father blamed me for her death. He knew that I was different, and knew that I have lived for centuries, believing that somehow, I could make his daughter well. But no matter what I tried, it didn't work.

"We have a war brewing that I don't know if we can win," I confide, knowing that I won't get a reply but feeling better for talking about it. The others are like my brothers. We have been together for centuries, looking out for each other no matter what, but sometimes I just need the quiet of my thoughts, the stillness of this place.

Sighing, I open my eyes, looking around at the beauty that surrounds me. Spring has come early, and the meadow is blooming with flowers. The trees that surround this small piece of heaven stifle the sounds of the cars in the distance, giving me a moment in time to forget about all the trouble which we have had, all the trouble that is coming.

If it were only the gangs, we would easily defeat them, but the gangs are being driven by a more powerful force. Just under a year ago we found out that Aldor, the CEO of Zorba Ltd, a conglomerate that concentrates its funds in generic drugs—a façade, because the real business is what they have been hiding.

Their experiments on humans try to enhance them—try to make them more like us. As Elementals, our senses are more attuned than humans, we are stronger, faster, and can bend the elements. I am a water bender, there are others that bend fire, air, and earth, and very few that bend more than one. The older the Elemental, the more powerful he is.

Zorba is experimenting on humans to give them our powers, and somehow, they are using the women that they have been kidnapping to help them in these experiments.

We still don't know how the women factor in the experiments, but we are going to find out because any one of those women can be one of my brothers' mates. As elementals we are born knowing that sooner or later, we will turn Keres if we don't find our true mate. A Keres is an Elemental that the darkness in our soul overcomes the goodness in us—the light. If we find our mate, then she brings more light into our lives, which overpowers the darkness. Otherwise, we travel through life fighting the darkness from defeating us.

Our women are also gifted with powers of their own. All of them are human, but they are born with specific gifts that enhance our own powers. Aldor, the Zorba CEO, is a Keres. He is filled with darkness, and even though a few years ago, after centuries of the Elementals fighting for our sanity, Draco, the President of the Elementals MC in Nature Valley, announced that his men had found a way of keeping the darkness at bay.

Ever since then, we Elementals go into the program.

If we find that we can't fight the darkness anymore and find that it's overriding our efforts then we are treated, staying in the compound until we feel normal again and the darkness has somehow retreated again. We started capturing all the Keres and placing them in the program once the Elementals that were in higher risk had been treated. With the Keres it allows for the darkness in them to be compressed so that their light can fight for a while longer as they continue looking for their mates.

I was one of the Elementals that was placed in the program when it was first launched, Tor forced me to go and get treated, he refused to let me turn, or take my own life as so many of us do when we don't want to turn dark. Tor is our leader, the President of the Cape Town Chapter, and even though he can be a real motherfucker when riled, I know that I can always depend on him.

He was trying to keep me sane, but I am tired. It has been centuries, and I am still fighting. Contrary to the others, I don't expect to find my mate. I believe that the woman I was supposed to be with has died and there was nothing I could do about it. She might not have been my true mate, but she made me laugh, and made me happy.

I hear a faint rustle in the distance and know that

someone is approaching. Closing my eyes again, I sigh. A few minutes later, I sense Garth's energy. It will be a bit before he reaches me, giving me a few more minutes of peace. "I have to go." I know that it's crazy to sit here and talk to a tomb, a tomb that after all these years has nothing more than bones, but I feel a need to share what is happening with Isabela.

When I sense Garth getting closer, I open my eyes, looking towards where I know he is approaching from. Garth is a big son of a bitch, usually easy going until angered, then it's a real problem to hold him back. Garth is the mediator among us, but he will be the first one in a fight if he sees an innocent in danger, or one of the MC brothers. Now, by the scowl on his face, I know that I am not going to like what he has to say.

"Why the fuck aren't you answering your phone?" his deep voice booms across the meadow. His long, light brown hair has been tied up in a bun on the top of his head. Some of the guys tease him about his hair and how one of these days someone is going to confuse him for a woman, but it's only teasing because there is no way that anyone can ever confuse the man that is approaching with a woman.

"Maybe, did you ever think it was because I didn't want to be disturbed," I reply sarcastically in frustration. Is it too hard to ask for a little peace and quiet? As the enforcer for the Cape Town Chapter, I am responsible for making sure that we are safe at all times, that there are no threats, but how am I supposed to do that when we are at war?

I used to love the fighting, love being in the middle of a squabble. As Elementals, we are warriors— warriors that will fight until our last breath for what we believe. The only problem with me is that I don't know what I believe in anymore. When I look at this war we are in with the gangs, I know that it's because of the women that they are kidnapping, because of Dag's woman, Esmeralda.

And even though I will always fight to keep any of my brother's mate's safe, I get tired of always fighting for a lost cause. It seems that as soon as we conquer one problem, then another one is growing somewhere else. Evil seems to procreate faster than we can stop it. I shake my head at the thoughts that are running through it.

"We had a meet; you were supposed to be there," Garth states as he comes to stand before me, his body blocking out the sun. Shit, why the fuck would we have a meeting out of the blue?

"What for?" I ask, raising a brow as Garth places his hands low on his waist.

"We are leaving for Qatar."

"What?" shit, I should really have been at the fucking meeting. We know that Aldor is transporting women to Qatar, and that Zorb headquarters are in Qatar, but I didn't think we would be the ones going to Qatar.

"Yeah, we're leaving tomorrow morning," Garth says as he steps to my side and takes a seat on the ground, his back also leaning against the corner of the Tombstone.

"Why the fuck are we going? Why aren't Draco's men going or the guys from the Johannesburg chapter?" Raising my hand, I slide my fingers through my dark hair, feeling the slight sting as my hair pulls at my skull, welcoming the slight twinge of pain.

"Draco's men are all mated, and the Johannesburg guys seem to have a problem of their own down there, seems like they are coming down with different ailments."

I turn my head to look at him. "What the fuck are you talking about? We don't get sick." The human ailments have never affected us, as our Immune systems are stronger, more averse to any sickness that the humans catch.

"Apparently they are getting sick, Bion has gone there to see what the fuck is happening." Bion is a healer in our Mother Chapter, a great healer that we all turn to when encountering a problem.

"Who is going?" We can't all go to Qatar with a war going on here, but what Garth says is true. The Nature Valley chapter, our mother chapter, we can't expect any of the men from there to go unless they take their mates with them. When an Elemental mates, he can't stay away from his mate for very long as both him and his woman will start feeling withdrawal symptoms. Mates must touch frequently, or they suffer the same as a human does when someone close to them dies.

Mates can't live without each other, and that is why when one of them dies, the other one soon follows. If it's the woman dying and the elemental doesn't take his own life, then he turns Keres and will need to be put down.

"You…"

The word has me grunting in reply.

"Me, Asgar, Einar, and Colborn."

"Tor isn't going?" I ask, surprised not to hear his name.

"Because of the war here, everyone thought it best

for him to stay, also as Draco says, we don't know what we are walking into, we need him here to move more men if we need them," Garth updates. I can just imagine that Tor wasn't at all happy at having to stay behind.

"Draco was at the meeting?"

"No, he phoned in."

I nod in acknowledgment of his reply.

"They want intel. They don't expect us to interact with anyone yet."

"We are taking Colborn to get intel?" I ask with a raised brow. Colborn is hot tempered and hard to control. He is a violent son of a bitch, deadly in a fight, and one of the best men to have your back, but he is not the man to take with you if you're not expecting to fight.

"We needed a fire element in the group, Ulrich is mated so he can't go, and Tor is staying behind." Garth replies with a shrug.

"How are we getting in?" Qatar isn't the easiest countries to get in with weapons, especially if we don't want anyone to know that we are there.

"It has been arranged for us to hide in a cargo plane that is leaving early tomorrow morning. When we get there, we are to meet Mohamad. He will get us out of the airport and to where we will be staying for the length of our stay."

"And how long is that supposed to be?" I ask, already dreading the stay there. I have been to Qatar before, as a matter of fact, I have been to every country at one time or another throughout my very long five hundred and twenty-six years, and Qatar isn't a country that I would like to go back to.

"As long as it takes." Garth grunts, telling me that he too would rather not be going. His hazel eyes snap to mine as he inclines his head towards the tombstone behind us. "Why are you here?" he asks, which has me sighing.

"Just needed some peace." I reply with a shrug, not wanting to bare my heart to anyone. I know that whatever I tell Garth would stay between us unless he was worried about me, but I would rather not burden him with my demons, knowing that he will carry his own without having to listen to mine.

"You know I'm always here if you want to talk," he mutters and then grins. "And I answer back."

"Yeah, yeah, very funny," I mutter as I stand, ready to make my way back to the club. If we are leaving tomorrow, there is a lot to prepare before leaving.

SIENA 2

Opening my eyes, I wince at the pain that shoots up my back. Will this constant prodding ever end? "Siena?" I realize now that the whisper of my name is what woke me up. I start to turn my head, only to wince again as the pain intensifies. Shit, what did they do to me this time?

"Yes?" I'm not even sure if my voice was loud enough for Amber to hear me.

"Are you okay?" she asks.

I don't know what to reply. Am I okay? I don't even know how long I have been here for, how long they have been running tests on me. Damn ice-cream! If it wasn't for my sweet tooth, they might never have picked me to kidnap.

"I don't know." I wish I knew what they wanted, and why they are doing all these tests on us. I feel like I have been here for months, but one day is pretty much like any other, and they seem to roll together. The good thing is that they should be leaving me alone for a while. I also know from experience that they won't be giving me anything for the pain.

"What did they do this time?" The question comes from the other side of my glass cell from Liria, and as far as we know, the youngest among all of us. Liria is only eighteen, while I am twenty-six and Amber is twenty-nine.

"Something to… argh," I whimper as I try to move, and the pain radiates right through me. When the pain starts to alleviate somewhat, I continue, "the pain is on my back, I don't know what they did."

"Maybe they did the same to you as they did to Daria. Remember? She had that metal mechanism placed on her spine," Amber suggests, which has me squeezing my eyes tight. "Maybe try to feel with your hand if you can feel anything."

There is no way that I am moving my arm, leg, or any other part of me at the moment, as the pain is excruciating. "Not now," I whisper, taking in a breath to try to calm myself. If my muscles are relaxed, then the pain shouldn't be so bad.

I hear Amber say something else, but I don't pay attention as I try to relax my body, my mind wandering as I try to forget the pain and think of anything else but the horror of what I am living in this moment in my life. Just before I was taken, I booked to go to the hairdresser. I wanted a change, complaining constantly that my life was becoming monotonous. We as humans never appreciate what we have. It's only when we lose it that we realize what we have lost.

I would give anything right now to go back to my empty little flat, my job as a personal assistant to the most demanding man I have ever met, and just live my monotonous life without all this pain and uncertainty of when they will decide to kill us off.

My parents must be worried about me, frantic to know what has happened to their daughter. I phone them every Friday without fail. How many Fridays has it been now without a call from me? I am sure they would have called the cops by now, but it will be to no avail, because one thing I know is that I am no longer in South Africa as they had us transported on a ship.

When I was brought here, there was another girl with me, but she isn't in here where the rest of us are. Our cells are made of glass and only a couple of feet in width with a metal slab that works as our bed and toilet at the opposite side of the door.

At the beginning, going to the toilet with all the other women being able to watch me was a problem, but as time passed, we got used to it. Once every five days we are taken one at a time to shower, but otherwise, our entertainment is sitting in this glass cage looking at each other. There is nothing for us to do, no exercise to have except if we pace our cells, which are only a couple of feet each way.

There are eighteen women here at the moment, and some of them were already here when I came. There are others that came after me, but one thing we all know is that when they come for us, we might never come back. There have been at least three that haven't made it back, three that we are certain that they have died while they do their experiments on us.

It's clear that they don't expect us to ever leave here, as most of the men that bring us food don't wear face coverings. I have also noticed that they call us by numbers instead of names. At first, I used to scream and bitch as someone came into view, but as time passed, I realized that they didn't pay us any attention.

When I was first kidnapped, I was scared, because being diabetic I was certain that once they found out they would either kill me or let me go. Instead, they kept me, and I sometimes wished for death instead of what they do to me. I thought that they were trafficking me into the sex trade, but I think this is much worse. These men and women are heartless. They do all these tests on us, without any type of anaesthetic, without any type of pain killers.

At the beginning they stopped giving me insulin

until I nearly died, but then they started to inject me again. Why? Why would they want to keep me alive when they can just pick up other women somewhere?

"Siena!"

My name being called brings me back to the present—to the excruciating pain.

"Let me sleep."

"Sorry, I'm just worried about you," Amber says. She has told me about her life, about how they found her in a woman's shelter. She has had a bad time of it. It's unfair that when she finally thought that she was safe, these assholes kidnap her and make her suffer some more. I slowly start to turn my head; every inch of movement is like a knife stabbing into my back, but after what feels like hours, I am looking at Amber through the glass that separates our cells.

Her shoulder length, honey coloured hair is falling around her face, covering her pixie expression, and the scar that she has across her jaw and cheek. Her big blue eyes focused on me, a worried expression on her face. "It's going to be okay. Just hang in there. Don't give up, it's going to be okay." I don't know if she is trying to convince me or herself.

"I'm so tired of these constant tests," Liria murmurs.

"The best you can do is relax between what they do to you, try to heal, regain your strength, and hope that soon someone will come looking for us," Anabelle says. She is one of the women that has been here the longest. Sometimes at night I hear her moan in pain, but she never shows her weakness to any of us.

"I would love to know before I die, what they are trying to accomplish with all these experiments they do on us?" Amber questions in a quiet voice, and I am sure it is something that every one of us would like to know. This is like being in prison but worse, at least in prison you get to go out into a courtyard—get to enjoy the weather.

In here, we don't know if it's raining or sunshine, and they give us the same food every day. I feel a tear slip down my cheek. I always think I have exhausted all my tears, but they manage to wring more out of me. I wish my gift hadn't deserted me now. Ever since I was born, I could charge anything with electricity. While other people are scared of getting electrocuted, current does nothing to me. When my parents found out about my gift, they took me for various tests, nothing like the ones being done on us now. They told me at the time that

I am like an electric conductor. I would gladly electrocute every person that has hurt us, every person that hasn't done anything to help us when they knew what we are going through.

Now when I most need my gift, it has gone away. It has left me, like my life will eventually leave me too if I stay here much longer. All I know is that I can't take much more of these experiments, I can't take much more pain.

My back feels like I have a bar of metal entwined in my spine. Even if we ever got out of here, how would we be able to live in the real world? I'm sure that our bodies won't survive for very long after everything we have gone through here. At least I have met some really great women, because even though most of the time we are all in pain, we support each other through the horrors that we are living.

I hear the door opening and tense, only to cry out when pain radiates through my body. Footsteps approach, but I can't turn my head to see, so I look at Amber to gage her reaction. By the fear in her eyes, it's clear that it's one of the men that takes us away. Surely, they're not going to work on anyone else today.

Then the footsteps stop, and I swear it sounds like it's right outside my door. Amber's eyes snap to mine and widen. Then they are turning again towards whoever is in the corridor. There is a snap, and a door is being opened, and then I see a hand next to my head. "What, what is…" my next words are a scream as whoever is in the room turns me on my side.

My vision blurs as the pain overwhelms me, and I feel myself falling into a merciless oblivion.

***

I don't know how long it is before I awaken again, but all I know is that when I open my eyes, it's not the usual glass walls that I see. Instead, I am looking at a white wall. The pain is still as bad as before, which leads me to believe that it hasn't been a long time since they took me from the glass cell.

Why have they brought me here? Are they going to experiment on me again? Surely not. I doubt I will be able to withstand any more pain besides what I am already feeling. I start to turn my head once again, slowly to the other side, so I can see where I am. The tears run down my cheeks at the pain of moving my head and what it does to my back, but I persist. The room is similar to the one I had in glass, except this one has real walls and contrary to the glass cells where they had cameras high up in the warehouse ceiling, here there is a camera in the corner of the room.

Are they monitoring me? It's silly because I wouldn't be able to move even if I wanted to. Are they going to kill me? The questions keep shooting through my mind relentlessly until they are interrupted by a sound, and then I see a figure appear from behind me. This man must be in his forties and by the white coat he is wearing, I would say he is some kind of doctor.

"Hello, Siena."

"You know my name?" they have never asked for my name, not from the moment I was kidnapped, and instead have called me by a number when referring to me.

"Yes, and now I know a little more about you. You surprised me, I never thought we would have such a little firecracker among us."

His reply has me confused. *What does he mean firecracker?*

"I don't understand." That's an understatement. Since the day they took me, I haven't understood anything.

"Let's just say that you are going to become very useful once you heal from this latest testing. Then we will start measuring your full potential." He steps closer and now I see him clearly, his dark brown hair streaked with white just over his temples, his eyes reminding me of a snake when they are about to strike. His eyes are running up and down my body as he shakes his head as if in surprise. "Amazing, such a little thing with so much potential."

Before I can ask him what he is talking about, he steps away, and I hear what sounds like a door closing. What did he mean? Does that mean that they aren't going to kill me? I am so tired. I wish I could close my eyes and when I open them again, all of this was a nightmare. But nightmares don't hurt physically as much as I am hurting.

I always wanted a child—a family that I could call my own and cherish, but that dream has vanished with each experiment they did on me. Everything they have done to me is inhuman, things that no one would ever think happen in this day and age, but they do. The intense evil in this place is palpable, and it is consuming me with each slice of their blade on my body.

There are two women in the glass cells which they have experimented with their brains. It is clear by the way they now act that the experiment has affected them intensely because sometimes they seem to be completely out of it. I don't know how many women have passed through those cells, but I hope that everyone responsible pays dearly for what they have made us suffer.

EIRIK 3

Keeping to the shadows, we make our way towards the darkened building. Arriving in Qatar a week ago, we went around finding as much information as possible without raising suspicion. Zorba Industries is a huge plant with different warehouses all over the property. Without actually breaking in and looking into what they are keeping inside, we won't be able to tell what they are doing.

So, we have looked at the building plans and every flaw that we could find in their security. Colborn and I are making our way into one of their side buildings, a building that looks like it could hold their labs. The last thing I feel like is going through reams and reams of papers trying to find any indication that they are up to something here.

Colborn points to the top of the building.

Looking up, I see the camera and nod as we continue to make our way in the shadows until we reach the sewer cover. Colborn is already bending over it to lift the lid so that we can slide into the opening and make our way inside the building through here. We continue in silence until we reach the point below the building that has a cover above us that we know leads to the room where they hold all the generators.

Lifting the cover as quietly as possible, we lift ourselves into the machine room. Looking around, we see nothing to worry about here, and it seems like no one is working at this time. It was just as we hoped, because we were thinking of using the same route as an exit. I listen to the different sounds, and by the footsteps and voices I hear, I would say there are at least three men to our right on the same floor as the machine room.

I incline my head towards the electrical board, knowing that soon the generators will kick in when Colborn melts some of their wires, but the cameras won't come on with the generator power because that main switch will be one of the wires affected.

Colborn opens the board and looks around at all the switches before he finally finds the ones he was looking for as he pulls open the plastic covers. Placing his hand over the cables, he looks at me and winks. A minute later smoke starts to rise from where his hands are, and then a blazing fire. The smell of melting plastic permeates the air. Colborne places the covers back before turning to me.

I point up, indicating that we should make our way to the top floor. Walking towards the door, I slide it open and look out, then up and down the corridor just as all the lights go off.

"Better hurry before the sprinklers kick in," Colborne says as we hurry towards the stairs that lead to the first floor.

Opening the door, I stop. There seems to be quite a few people on this floor, but it is deathly quiet. Stepping into the corridor, I start heading right, while Colborn turns left, making his way towards where we were told the offices were. He will find the server, place the USB that Celmund sent us and follow instructions so that Celmund can penetrate their files without anyone knowing.

Walking up to the first door, I slide it open, looking inside to see a lab with a couple of microscopes and test tubes that are all placed neatly inside a fridge. Maybe this is where they test the new generic medication they produce?

Walking back out, I head to a door further up and opposite where the lab is, only to frown when I open the door. Now why the hell would they have operating rooms in here? Walking inside, I look around to find everything sterilized and no evidence of what they might use this room for.

Pulling out my phone, I take photos so that we can send all the info we gather to the place we are holed up at. Walking out, I make my way down the corridor looking into other areas, but all seem like they are testing medication, that is, except for the operating room.

At the end of the corridor, I see a keypad next to a door. Looking through the small window I see at least eight doors closer together. Now why would those doors be protected by a security pad. Placing my hand flat on the door where the lock is located, I give it one firm push, and it pops open with a cracking sound.

"What the fuck are you doing, we're not supposed to leave evidence that we were here," Colborne says from behind me.

"Why do you think they would need the extra security?" I ask as I glance back at Colborn. "I think they are trying to hide something.

"It doesn't feel right in here," Colborn mutters as we step inside.

I know what he means because the hair at the back of my neck is standing up on end, and I have an unsettling feeling.

"Take the right and I will look left," I say.

Colborn is already approaching the small window to the door on the right. I start to approach the one on the left when I hear Colborn startled yelp.

"What the fuck?" Looking back, I see him a few steps away from the window. On the other side of the door is a woman, or I think it's a woman. Her forehead is against the glass and her glazed milky white eyes are staring straight at Colborn.

"Well, I guess we know what's behind that door," I reply, looking back towards my door and approaching cautiously. I guess if you have someone suddenly appear on the other side of the door, anyone would get a fright.

Looking into the room, I see a woman sitting cross legged on a metal slab, her long white, blonde hair seems to be floating around her and she seems to be meditating. Lifting my phone I take a photo. I guess we found the women. Lowering my phone, I step back, moving towards the next door.

Now I know why we were feeling so unsettled. If we are right, then all the women in these rooms have special gifts, and if they are anything like Freya, Anastasia, and Esmeralda, their gifts are amazing. When Dane, Ulrich, and Dag mated it was interesting to get to know their mates and the way their gifts enhanced the men's. It has also brought some semblance of normality to the club, even though Tor is fighting hard to stop the change. I shake my head, thinking of the crazy parties and eccentric items Tor used to purchase before.

He has accepted all three women into our club, our family, but it is clear that he is struggling with the change of being more restrained. Looking into the next room. I am in a way disappointed not to see anyone, but in another, glad because it means they don't have a woman locked up against her will. "I will be back to help you, I promise," I hear Colborn saying, but I don't look back as I approach the next door.

Approaching the glass, I get a feeling of urgency, like I need to hurry. These rooms seem to be soundproof because otherwise, these women would have heard us coming. Looking inside, I see a woman sitting on the floor with her head thrown back as she leans against the bed, looking up at the ceiling while her auburn hair flows around her. I place the palm of my hand flat on the door as I look at her. Suddenly, she starts to turn her head towards me. When her eyes connect with mine, I freeze.

Her green eyes feel like they penetrate right into my soul, her sad expression wrenching at my heart. I see her frown and she slowly raises her head, her movements sluggish. She moves her lips, but I can't tell what she is saying. I need to get her out of here. I need to help her.

Her hand rises, and she holds out her palm like she

wants to touch mine. Everything within me calls to this woman, calls to the pain, and the sorrow that she is feeling. "I will help you! I will come back and get you out of here," I mouth. "Do you understand?"

She lowers her hand to the ground beside her, and then lays her head back again, closing her eyes.

"Look at me," I call, but she doesn't turn her head again. I feel like I have let her down, like I have abandoned her. My heart is racing, my mouth feels dry, and my head is pounding.

"Eirik?" Colborn calls. But I ignore him as I fight this feeling of urgency within me to protect this woman. "Eirik?" Colborn places his hand on my shoulder, shaking me. "What the hell is wrong with you, we don't have all night."

"I'm taking her!" I can't leave her here. She is clearly in pain, and I need to help her.

"You're not taking anyone; you think I don't want to take all of them with me? But there might be more, and we need help to get as many of them out of here and home before they move them or kill them. Look at me!" I know that what he is saying is true, but I can't leave her here. "Eirik!"

"She's mine!" The words seem to have been

wrenched out of my soul. Is that possible? Is she really mine? The urgency I feel, the overwhelming sense of desperation to free her.

"Fuck me!" Colborn grunts as he lifts his phone to his ear.

"We have a major fucking problem," he says into the phone. I know he has to be phoning Tor, and that what he said earlier is true. If I take her, we might not be able to save the other women because they might take them away or kill them before we can get to them. But how can I leave her here? How can I…

"Here, Tor wants to talk to you."

I take the phone, continuing to look at the woman sitting on the floor. Her head is still laying back against the bed, her eyes still closed, completely ignoring me.

"Yeah?"

"Are you sure?" Tor's question has me grunting. What does he think? He would know that from all the men I would never admit to a mate unless completely certain.

"Yeah."

"If you break her out now, we might lose all the

other women. I will get all the MC ready, and we will be there by tomorrow morning. We need to bring back as many women as we can Eirik, we need to make sure that we help them." I know that what he is saying is true, but I don't think I can leave her here. Everything in me is screaming for me to ignore everything else and just take her away to freedom, take her away from everything. "Eirik?" Tor snaps.

"Yeah?"

"Let me talk to Colborn." Handing the phone to Colborn, I take in a deep breath wishing that I could take in her essence.

"We need to go. I have taken photos of all the women in the other rooms. Tor says we will be back tomorrow." Colborn once again places his hand on my shoulder, squeezing in understanding. "You need to do this Eirik, she will be fine until tomorrow."

"How do you know that?" They might come in and kill her before I can come back. I can't let that happen.

"There is a schedule on that desk. Room three, which is this one, has nothing scheduled until two weeks from today. Room eight is the one that is scheduled tomorrow at one in the afternoon, so we better fucking be here before that, because I told her I would help her out."

I take in a deep breath, raising my phone so I can take a photo of the woman. I don't even know her name.

"Did the schedule have her name?"

"No, just numbers," Colborn replies as he starts making his way towards the door I opened.

"Shit, we need to fix this, or they will know we were here." I look at the door, it seems fine except for the bracket where the lock slots in.

"I will melt the fucking steel slightly. Should hold it so we can close the door again." He takes the bracket in his hand. A few minutes later the bracket is red hot as he places it in place.

"Someone is coming. We need to hurry," I warn as I hear the footsteps approaching.

Colborn pulls the door shut, holding it a few seconds before letting go. We both breathe out in relief when the door holds shut.

"Let's hide in there, it's a lab," Colborn calls as he heads towards two doors down. We are just closing the door quietly after us when the footsteps stop.

"The machine rooms?" we hear someone saying. "We just had a check done on that board." He starts walking again, but this time the footsteps are receding. "I'm coming down."

I incline my head towards the door. Time to get out of here. We need to get to the kitchen and out through there.

We head in the direction we know the kitchen is at. Each step closer to the kitchen is a step further from my woman. The thought still doesn't seem to register. After all these years thinking that Isabella was the only woman for me—thinking that no matter what, I didn't want a mate. Now here I am obsessed with saving her from this hell hole.

I'm a protector, a warrior against injustice and evil. That must be why I have this driving force to take her to safety. She might be my mate, but I doubt she will ever make me as happy as Isabela did.

SIENA 4

I don't know how long it has been since they experimented with my back, but the pain is taking long to recede. It must have been days, or maybe just hours. Ever since I was taken, I don't seem to know day from night. At least now I can move, but very slowly. I have found that I rest better sitting on the floor with my head leaning against the metal frame of the bed. It supports my head, which currently feels too heavy for my body.

The food is brought in and then taken out; I try to eat but after a few bites my arms are just too heavy for me to lift. The man that came to see me when I was first brought into this room hasn't been back, therefore I still don't know what he meant.

What I do remember is the dream, or maybe it was a vision I had of a man standing by the door looking at me. He somehow feels familiar. His shocked expression seemed sad. I wanted to take him in my arms and hold him close until the sadness went away, which is silly because if anyone needs to be held close it's me. I swear he mouthed that he was going to come back to help me, which proves that it must have been a dream, because why wouldn't he just take me away when he saw me?

At least I have dreams of hot, badass looking guys. How did I even conjure him up in my dream? Must have been someone I saw sometime while out and didn't even realize I had seen him. I think back to Jack. He definitely didn't look like that. I was seeing Jack for two-and-a-half years when I found out that he was cheating.

I thought I loved him. I thought we would be married one day and live happily ever after. Looks like I thought a lot of things that didn't happen. And now they will never happen because as soon as I found out that Jack was cheating, I stopped seeing him—stopped taking his calls. I don't believe him. No matter how much he tried to convince me that he loved me, he still cheated.

Someone that loves you doesn't sleep with someone else. I thought we were fine. I thought we had something good going, but apparently, I wasn't good enough if he needed to find another woman to sleep with. When I found out, he tried to tell me that it was a moment of temptation and that it would never happen again. He said he was drunk, and she threw herself at him. But how would I know that it would never happen again?

When that happened, I was devastated. But with time, I realized that I wasn't upset about losing him, but upset over the death of my dream—the death of that perfect life that I imagined with him. In reality, I actually wasn't at all upset at not seeing him any longer, which gave me a moment of pause. What if I had gone ahead and married him? What if after being married for a couple of years I discovered that I didn't love him but the idea of what I could have with him?

Now I will never know. I will never be able to have that dream but instead live this nightmare every day. Turning my hands, I place my palms down on the ground as I prepare to move slowly, because my ass is starting to feel numb. I freeze when I start feeling a familiar current under my fingertips. It is slight, but it is there. Is it possible? Am I feeling electric currents again?

Why did it go away, and why is it now coming back? Did they somehow drug me? I didn't even think about the possibility that they are drugging us and that is why I wasn't able to feel the current. I have so many questions and no one to answer them.

One thing I do know is that at least now I can try to defend myself. Now it won't be as easy for them to hurt me again. I am in pain, and can hardly move, but for the first time since my abduction, I have hope.

I will need to bide my time because there is no way

that I can run away from here. But maybe I can when I am feeling better and if I ever move normally again. I will try my luck at running. I would love to help the other women. I want to help Amber and Liria and the others to escape, but I don't even know where they are or where we are being kept. Maybe we are out of town, and I will have to hide while I make my way to safety, or maybe we are in the middle of a city, and I will be able to find help easily.

I will have to contact the authorities and my parents. I smile. I would shake my head if it wasn't so painful. I'm making all these plans when all I felt was a slight current. I feel a sense of foreboding telling me that someone is watching me. Turning my head, I tense when I see two men with white coats at the open door looking at me.

"She also looks the same," one of them says as he writes something on his clipboard. "The generators kicked in, so there wouldn't have been a big lag until everything came back on."

"You think she did it?" the other one asks as they both look at me.

What do they think I did when I can't even move?

"No, even though we have reduced her medication it is still prohibiting her full functions." So, it is true, they are drugging me. That's why I haven't been able to feel the current. Maybe I should stop eating, because that is the only way I imagine they are getting their drugs into me, but if I stop eating all together, I will be too weak to do anything, anyway.

I feel so helpless, why would anyone do this to another human being. They close the door again and everything quietens once again. The only sound is the very slight buzzing of the camera when it turns with my movements. Suddenly, something they said dawns on me. They know. They know about me conducting energy.

Is that why they took me? Is this all about what I can do? But what about the others? Can they also conduct electricity like I do? I never for once thought about that. It is possible that there are more people out there that do the same as me. There is no reason why it would only be me. Sighing, I lay my head back again. I have so many unanswered questions.

***

I must have fallen asleep because suddenly I am startled awake, crying out as I jerk in pain when I try to move my head. What woke me up? I am so stiff from sitting like this in the same position that I don't know how long it will take me to straighten up. The cold from the ground penetrates my bones, making it even more painful.

Then I hear a noise. Someone is at the door again. Luckily, my head is already slightly turned that way. Opening my eyes, I see movement through the little window as if someone is there and then there is a loud cracking sound, and the door is opening. My eyes widen when I see the man of my dreams standing in the opening.

Am I dreaming again? Damn, whatever they are giving me, maybe they should continue?

"I came back."

Wait, he spoke.

"Why are you still on the floor?" His voice is deep. There is an inflection of concern in his voice as he steps closer. He is bigger and more handsome than I first thought. If this is a dream, then please don't let it end.

"Are you real?"

At my question, he nods as he squats down before me. I hear noise outside in the corridor, but I don't look. Instead, I keep my eyes on him in case he disappears again.

"I came to take you away from here." Is he the grim

reaper? Because there is no way an angel of mercy would look like him. There are tattoos running up his neck, down his arms, and on his knuckles. The only place I think this man doesn't have tattoos is his face.

"Are you going to kill me?" Has this horror finally come to an end?

But my question has a look of horror fill his expression, and I see his muscles tensing.

"We need to hurry this up," someone calls from the doorway.

"Coming," he says, and I see his arms stretching out to lift me, which has me cringing immediately at the thought of the pain that will assault me at the movement.

"I'm not going to hurt you," he says as he stops just before he touches me.

"Yes, you are," I reply.

He shakes his head as he gently slides his one arm under my legs, even the slight movement has sharp pain rushing up my legs and lodging in my back, but I bite down on my lip, not wanting to stop him in case he leaves me behind. But when his arm slides behind my back, I can't hold the cry in.

"Fuck," he grunts as he freezes, "where does it hurt?"

I want to answer but can't because I'm trying to control the pain, so that I don't lose consciousness.

"Talk to me. Where does it hurt?"

I squeeze my eyes shut, taking in a deep breath to try to push down the sharp pains.

"Bion!" he suddenly roars, which has my eyes snapping open.

His head is turned towards the door, his arms are still in place, but he hasn't lifted me yet. Instead, he is tensed as if ready to spring. I can't see his expression, but there is a muscle twitching at his jaw professing his anger.

"What?" someone asks.

"She's in pain," my saviour says.

"Yeah, it seems like they all are. These motherfuckers were experimenting with them." This man comes into my line of vision, and if it wasn't for the pain, I would definitely believe that I was dreaming. This guy looks like a surfer if I ever saw one, but he has the kindest eyes as he looks down at me.

"Sweetheart, have they given you anything for pain?" He goes down on his knees next to my saviour while he waits for my reply.

"No." My reply has the other man swearing angrily.

"Motherfuckers, what's the point of keeping them in pain?"

"Where does it hurt, sweetheart?" Bion asks.

"Everywhere," I answer again, even though now that my saviour isn't moving, the pain is starting to diminish.

"Do you know why it hurts everywhere?"

"My back."

I feel my saviour's arms tense.

"Don't move," Bion says as he suddenly lies down next to me and then starts to slide under the metal bunk and behind me. I feel light fingers lifting the flaps of the coat that I am using. "Carefully move your arm further up," Bion calls from where he is.

My saviour's arm starts to move, and even though he tries to be as gentle and as slow as possible, it still jolts me slightly, which has me gulping in pain. I once again feel the flaps of the coat parting and then the light touch of Bion's fingers.

When he slides out from under the bed, I see his expression has darkened in anger. He leans towards where he dropped a haversack near my saviour before he went to examine me. "I'm going to give you something for the pain. It will put you to sleep but it will help."

"What did they do?" I ask, knowing that it can't be good, but hoping that it won't be permanent.

"I can't really tell until I examine you more thoroughly, but believe me when I say that the pain will stop now," he says this as he starts to inject something into my arm.

"Thank you." I don't care what he gives me. If it takes the pain away, I will be forever thankful. I see Bion and my saviour look at each other, and then Bion is inclining his head towards me.

"You can move her when she has fallen asleep, not before." And just as he says that, I can feel my eyes start to shut, the darkness of unconsciousness pulling me in. My body seems to be floating and I realize that for the first time in a very long while, I am not feeling pain.

"What is your name, sweetheart?" Bion asks.

"Se…" I start to say, but my lips and brain don't cooperate as I let sleep take hold of me. Before I lose complete consciousness, I feel strong arms lift me, and then I'm being held carefully against warmth that soothes my cold body.

"I won't let anyone ever hurt you again."

Those whispered words from my saviour are what finally lulls me into oblivion.

EIRIK 5

Every nerve ending in my body is screaming for revenge. I saw Bion's expression after he looked at my woman's back, and I can tell that whatever they did appalled him. I want to kill every son of a bitch that did this to her. I felt helpless when she cried out in pain, an emotion that I promised myself I would never feel again.

Every abled man in the MC is here today to take away all the women that we possibly can. We would have liked nothing more than to kill Aldor while we are at it, but the son of a bitch isn't here. I can hear fighting and know that some of the others must have encountered the enhanced soldiers that this place has been producing. We will take as much information as we possibly can, because Zorba has more than one company, and we are aware that they might have this operation running somewhere else too, even though we think this is their main and biggest one.

Pulling my woman closer against me, I make my way out of the building and towards one of the trucks that we brought to take the women out of here, but when I reach it, I notice that it is full, and there are more women here than we thought. Moving towards another one where Hawk, one of the members from our Johannesburg chapter, is just now turning from helping a woman into it.

"Fuck, Brother, I have seen a lot of shit, but this is barbaric." In this truck the women seem to be doing a little worse than the others, but again there must be at least twenty women already in here. "We should burn this fucking place to the ground," he says angrily as he makes his way back into the building.

Bion is heading towards us with a woman in his arms and a scowl on his face. "We need more trucks; these aren't going to be enough," he states as he walks past me towards the third one. I follow to see this one is half full already.

"I'm going in here with her."

Bion looks back at me and nods, then points to me. "You need to bond with her, her healing will be quicker. Besides, you already touched her so there is no going back." He walks away after having his say, leaving me looking down at the woman that was chosen for me by fate.

She is beautiful, and even though she has been through hell, she hasn't given up. She feels so right in my arms but knowing that she is mine makes me feel guilty when I think of Isabela.

Her hair is flowing over my arm, her green eyes now closed with a slight sprinkle of freckles across the bridge of her nose. The deep protective feelings I have for her are unknown to me, but I think that is because she is hurt.

"You were unexpected," I whisper as I climb into the truck, seeing all the women's scared eyes focus on me.

"Siena?" a voice calls when I take a seat by the door. My gaze snaps up towards the women, to find the one that spoke.

A woman toward the back is looking at us with a worried expression on her face. "Is she okay?" she asks.

"What did you call her?" I ask, wanting to make sure that she is talking about the woman in my arms.

"Siena," she says again.

Siena! It's different, but I like it.

"I don't know yet; the healer will have to examine her first."

She nods, her hand raising to her chest. "I thought

she was dead when they took her away again. I thought they had killed her." Her voice is choked with emotion. "I am so relieved to know that she is still alive."

"How long has she been here?"

Another woman that is sitting closer to me replies. "We wouldn't know how long anyone has been here. We never saw the light of day."

Her words have my anger rising another notch. When I first touched her, her skin was ice cold, but now she has warmed up with the heat from my body. No one should ever go through what these women have gone through—the constant horror of what is going to be done to them.

"Are you taking us home?" another woman asks.

"Eventually. First, we will make sure you are all healed and feeling fine. Also, we need to make sure that this organization that found you won't come after you again. Once we know that you're safe, you can all go home."

"What's your name?" another woman asks.

"Eirik."

"Eirik, thank you." Those words make up for all the fighting and frustration we have endured all these years trying to stop the kidnapping of these incredibly special women.

"Do you know why they were experimenting with us?" the woman that gave me Siena's name asks.

"Because of the special gifts you all have. They are trying to enhance soldiers and using your gifts for it."

My statement has the women looking shocked, and then looking around. It seems like they were all keeping that from each other. It is a shame that in this world people still have to hide things like this from each other. The reason most of these women hid the fact that they have special gifts is so they aren't exploited for being different, or looked at differently. But even still they are hurt for being unique.

Looking out, I see the first truck pulling away just as Tal comes towards us with another woman in his arms. "Another one bites the dust," he teases as he sees Siena in my arms.

"I'm just helping her," I mutter, knowing that it's not true.

"Oh, if that is the case then I will sit here holding her while you go and see if there are any more women to bring out."

I growl instinctively, which has him grinning. The fucker was purposely baiting me, knowing that there is no way that I am going to pass my injured mate into anyone's arms.

"Piss off," I snap, just as I feel the ground shake.

Frowning, we both look at each other and then towards the building in the far corner where we felt the vibrations coming from.

"Someone is losing their shit. Hope it's not Draco," Tal says when there is another tremor.

"That's not strong enough to be Draco's," I reply.

Draco is the only Elemental we know that can bend all the elements, he is also the oldest of us, and the strongest. Before Draco found his mate, we all worried that one day he would turn and we would all have a hell of a time stopping him, but fortunately he hung in there, which professes to his inner strength.

The other truck pulls away, as Wulf, the Mother Chapter's VP, walks out the door of the closest building. "Clear," he calls.

We were hoping all to leave today, but there is no way that we can fly all these women out of Qatar today. Therefore, there will be some of us that will have to stay behind until they are all in safety. Also,

I don't think that all the women will be able to fly just yet. Looking down at my woman I tense. Her complexion is pale—paler than she was when I first brought her to the truck.

Leaning closer, I listen to her breathing—her heartbeat. The women are distracted, talking to each other about what they have just found out and not paying me any attention.

"I'm sorry Siena, I have to do this," I whisper against her ear as I pull out a blade that I have inside my boot. I slash my upper arm until there is blood dripping down it. Placing my arm over her mouth, I let the blood slide between her lips and into her mouth.

My wound is already closing and the blood stopping, but there was enough to start the transformation. Pulling her gently higher into my arms, I lower my head against her neck, her hair concealing my actions as I bite down on her shoulder. If bonding with Siena will save her life, then I will willingly do it. I will not have my mate suffer because of me.

The taste of her blood is as sweet as nectar, her taste an aphrodisiac that rushes through my bloodstream like an injection of passion. My body reacts with a burst of lust that leaves me stunned at its strength. I knew that mates had a unique bond that enhances their sexual encounters like nothing else can, but I never knew it was this strong.

Licking my lips, I raise my head to look down at my unconscious mate. I feel like a perv holding her injured body in my arms while my body fights its restraints, wanting to take her fully. My jeans feel too tight, as my cock twitches with exhilaration at finding its mate. My head might be telling me that I shouldn't be thinking of Siena like this, that I shouldn't want to bed her, but my body is thinking something else altogether.

"Clear," I hear Asgar call from one of the other buildings as Tor walks past him with a woman in his arms towards the truck. Everything about him exudes anger. It is clear that he is holding onto his fury by the skin of his teeth. Reaching the truck, he steps up and then slides down before me with the woman still in his arms.

"She okay?" I ask because she doesn't seem to be conscious. When my eyes rise to Tor's I am surprised to see the deep turmoil in his.

"She's alive." His eyes lower to Siena and then back up to mine. "She the one?"

"Yeah."

"Is she okay?" he asks as he looks at Siena again.

"They did something to her back. Bion gave her something for the pain and sleep. They make fucking pain killers, meanwhile they weren't giving them any after cutting them up." The anger in my voice is clear, but I whisper my words because I don't want the other women to hear our conversation.

"She's Haldor's sister."

I tense as my eyes snap down to the woman in Tor's arms.

"We had to knock him the fuck out when he saw her."

Now I realize that the tremors we felt earlier were from Haldor. Fuck, I knew he had a sister that was twenty something years old. We used to make fun of him when she was born, saying that she could call him grandpops instead of brother.

Haldor is young compared to most of us, with only two hundred and thirty years under his belt, but to have a sibling that is so much younger doesn't always happen. I remember him saying something about her studying to become a lawyer, and I know that even though he doesn't see her much, he has a soft spot for his little sister.

Seeing her here like this must have messed with his

mind. "Did he know she was missing?"

"No, so it was more of a shock when he's the one that fucking found her," Tor states angrily. "I would love to do to them what they have been doing to these women."

Haldor doesn't talk much and keeps his thoughts to himself. He's a deadly motherfucker and a sniper that never misses his target. I know that if he finds the fuckers that did this to his sister, he will go after them and to hell with everything else.

"It's going to be hard to stop him from going after them."

"We are all going to go after them. There is no way that we are going to sit back and let them continue their work somewhere else," Tor confides in me as he looks down at the woman that is starting to awaken.

"Does she know you?" I ask, as most of us at the club haven't met Haldor's sister yet.

"Yeah, I've seen her twice before."

"We are going to have to go to Zorba's other factories if this is what they are doing," I state as I look out to see two of the Johannesburg chapter brothers carrying two unconscious enhanced fuckers. All the men that we have managed to capture today will be questioned here, and then Draco will decide their fate. The mated men will be the first ones to fly out with the women that are stable enough to fly. The others will stay behind to secure the women that aren't yet ready to leave and to try to find the doctors that have been playing God with other human beings' lives.

"To... Tor?"

The whispered word has my eyes turning back to Tor and Haldor's sister.

"Yes, Darling, you're safe now." I have never heard that gentle tone in Tor's voice before. It is clear that he's livid about what has been going on here, but he is hiding it from this woman.

"Haldor?"

"He's fine. He will come to see you once you're settled. Now try to rest."

"Tor... I'm no... not going t... to make it."

Her broken words have my heart wrenching over the pain I hear in her voice.

"Nonsense, darling. We're not going to let anything happen to you," Tor says gently as she shakes her head tiredly.

"Tell Haldor... I love him."

"Rest, Darling, you will tell him yourself soon."

Her breathing is staggered, her heart rate slowing.

"Bion!" I call when I see him a couple of feet away. He turns at abruptly and then starts making his way towards us. When he is a couple of feet away, I incline my head towards Haldor's sister. I don't have to say anything, because Bion climbs into the truck and starts to examine the woman.

"Fuck, place her flat," Bion orders as he moves back to make space for the woman. As soon as Tor has her stretched out, Bion is over her. "Come on, sweetheart, don't give up now," he says in a gentle voice as he places his hand over her heart.

Tal climbs into the truck, closing the doors behind himself. "We are moving," he states.

"Are all the buildings clear?" Tor asks as Bion continues to examine the woman.

I turn my head towards Tal, giving Bion and Haldor's sister more privacy.

"No. The last and biggest building at the end hasn't been cleared, but Draco pulled most of us back because bombs have been triggered. We need to move because the mad motherfucker is going to blow the fucking place down," Tal updates.

"Shit." Tor stands as he moves towards the doors to open them again just as the truck starts moving.

"What are you doing?" I ask.

"I'm not going to leave anyone behind." And with those words he is jumping out of the truck, and I see he starts running towards the building at the end, which Tal reported on still not being cleared.

"Shit. Shit. Shit," I grunt as I stand. Turning, I gently place Siena flat on the ground. "Take care of my woman," I snap to Tal before I am jumping out of the truck, too. They are going to need water if the fucking place explodes, and I am going to make sure that we get as many people out of there as possible.

As I run towards the building, I see Draco Standing a couple of feet away, his arms are stretched out beside him as he opens his hands facing the building. Tor is nowhere to be seen, but Cassius, also a water bender from our Mother Chapter, and Einar are standing before the building with their hands outstretched as they bend all the water they can find in the building. If this fucking place explodes before we can clear it, at least it will be soaked inside and won't burn as intended.

Just then, Tor is rushing out with a woman in his arms, Burkhart from our Mother Chapter is right behind him with another. "There are five more inside," Burkhart calls out, which has me ignoring the danger as I run inside. I follow the sounds that are coming from the end of the second corridor. The ground is already all wet, the sprinkler system is spraying everything, and I can hear the pipes under the ground groaning at the rush of water.

Entering the room at the end of the corridor where I heard the screams, I see women huddling together. Why the hell aren't they running out if the door is open? Hurrying towards them, I realize that they are all tied down with chains.

Bending, I grab a chain and yank. The sound of plaster and brick snapping is loud in the room, but the main chain is out of the wall. Pulling the main chain free from the individual ones, I throw it into a corner. These women seem to be unharmed, except for their dirty clothes. "I need you to run," I roar just as an explosion rocks the building.

Too late.

I can feel the intensity of the explosion growing as it drives towards us. Closing my eyes, I stretch out my hands and envision water lifting all around us, filling this room, encasing us in a water bubble. I can feel the strength of the water rushing towards us. Because of the other water benders and the water that is already in the building, the pressure and amount of water is substantial and quickly surrounds us. I hear the women screaming, but I don't have time to appease them as I try to protect us as best as I can before we are all burnt to cinders.

Opening my eyes, I see the wall of fire surrounding us. The only thing holding it back is the water bubble we are in. Looking over my shoulder, I stare at the women that are looking around at each other, horrified. "Huddle together and follow me, stay close together."

They start to complain but I don't pay them any heed, as I need my full concentration on getting us all out of here alive. Envisioning the bubble widening into the corridor from which I came from, I start making my way back. It's a slow trek because the ground is already scorched and treacherous, but we need to hurry up before the building starts to give way and traps us in here.

The air is also starting to become a problem as the air inside the bubble is starting to diminish. The fire has sucked in all the oxygen, which becomes a problem for us. Visibility is also becoming a problem as I can't tell anymore where I'm going with the blazes. We make it another couple of feet before one of the women trips and we have to stop so that she can be helped up.

"I can't breathe," one gasps.

"We are nearly there," I lie, because I have no idea where the fuck we are. I make it another couple of feet before a torrent of water suddenly starts to flood the corridor, lifting us from the ground. There is only one person that would be able to move so much water at once. Draco must have located where we were and is now quenching the fire. Our path is practically opening up to a bed of wet, scorched tiles. As we see the door, Tor and Burkhart rush in to collect the women.

Turning, I start ushering them towards them. "Come on," I call to the last woman that seems to be afraid to leave. "It's okay, everything is going to be fine now." She slowly makes her way towards me just as I hear a loud crack overhead. I look up just as something hard hits me on the head, and then darkness is pulling me down into its grips.

SIENA 6

Ever since being saved from the clutches of madmen, I have existed on a cloud of painless bliss. For days, I have been surrounded by women that I had never seen before. Slowly, I saw the numbers start to dwindle until today, when I'm the one being transported into a plane. Instead of being happy that wherever they are taking me will be closer to home, I find myself in a panic—panicking that I might never see my saviour again.

He said no one would ever hurt me again, that he wouldn't let them. Where is he?

"Relax, everything is going to be okay."

Turning my head, I look at Tal. Ever since waking up from the injection Bion gave me the day I was taken from wherever I was being held, Tal has been by my side. He doesn't talk much except to make sure that I am fine.

"Where are you taking me?" I ask, for once hating this daze I am constantly in. I know that they are controlling my pain, but I hate feeling out of control.

"We are flying back to South Africa; you will be back on home soil soon."

Home? I can't even imagine going back to my old life, to that life that I just existed in instead of actually living. If this experience has taught me anything, it is to grab every opportunity with both hands and not let it go. To throw myself into whatever I want to do instead of being afraid of things that might never happen.

"Where is he?"

And there it is. I finally asked the question that has been plaguing me ever since I opened my eyes.

Tal might not even know who I am talking about, and I don't know what to call him because I never got his name.

Tal looks at me with an intense look. After a minute, he shrugs before answering. "He was injured the day we rescued everyone. It was only last night that he finally came back from being unconscious, and that was only for a couple of minutes."

He was injured? I feel a knot in my stomach as my heart starts to race.

"Is he okay?" *Why does the thought of him being injured frighten me so much?*

"Yeah, don't worry, he will be up and around in no time," Tal says before grinning. "Especially now."

I frown at his words. "What do you mean, how was he injured?"

Tal slides into the chair next to me. "Let's just say that I gave him some mate incentive." He grins at that before continuing. "There was an explosion in one of the buildings, when he was on his way out a beam collapsed and scrambled his brain, but as we all suspected, your man has found a reason to hang around, and has been holding on until the injury finally healed."

He said my man, but he can't possibly know who I am asking about, can he? "He's not my man!" I say, looking at him intently, wondering if I missed something in my daze.

Tal raises a brow, his grin widening. "That's where you are wrong, Red, you are very much his." And with those words he is standing and making his way towards the front of the plane.

What does he mean? Are we even talking about the same person?

I close my eyes, and the first thing that jumps into my mind is the image of my saviour. His sad eyes wrench at my heart, his touch gentle as he tried not to hurt me. If only what Tal said was true. I wouldn't look back. Instead, I would jump straight into my saviours' arms.

My mind is once again floating in a cloud of cotton. Whatever they have been giving me has helped with the pain because I don't feel any discomfort at all, but I sleep most of the time. I am nearly asleep when I feel someone taking my hand. Opening my eyes, I turn my head to come face to face with him.

"It's you," I whisper, worried that my mind is playing tricks on me, and then my eyes widen when I realize that he has a bandage around his head. "You are hurt!" Tal was telling the truth, and the man he was talking about is my saviour.

"I'll be fine, it's just a scratch." His voice slides over me like a hot summer breeze. I don't know what it is about him that soothes me, but he does. He is also the only man that has ever made my heart race. I have seen quite a few handsome looking men these last few days, as it seems like they were all thrown into the same area as me, but out of all of them his looks call to me, his dark blue eyes filled with so many secrets, have butterflies fluttering in my stomach.

I feel like a kid again, a kid that is experiencing her first crush for the first time, and with everything that has happened I do feel like I was reborn.

He raises his hand, stroking my cheek. The feeling is one of tenderness. "You are looking better. How are you feeling?" he asks.

"I haven't felt any pain at all. I have no idea if I'm better or worse. For now, I'm just riding this drug induced existence until I can move around."

He stops stroking my cheek to cup it as he looks intently into my eyes. "Have you been comfortable?"

Well, now that is an interesting question because everyone around me did everything they could to make me more comfortable. But with my back the way it is, it is still difficult to get comfortable most of the time.

"Everyone has been great; I have needed nothing. There is a guy you might know; his name is Tal." I feel his hand tensing against my cheek, but he doesn't move away. "He has always been there when I needed something."

He grunts, and then to my surprise, he suddenly lowers his head and kisses me.

I am so surprised at the gesture that at first, I just sit there like a vegetable, the taste of him somehow familiar to me. I might not be able to move much, but I will be damned if I am going to miss this opportunity of kissing this man back. When I finally get over my surprise and start kissing him, everything around us seems to vanish.

This man has some kind of hold on me, a hold that has every fibre in my being coming alive at his touch and his kiss. I have been kissed before, but never have I felt like I feel now. This is what a kiss is supposed to feel like, this complete and utter overwhelming of the senses. When every stroke of his tongue against mine is like the movement of two bodies against each other while they dance the tango.

We seem to be in sync with each other to a degree that I wouldn't be surprised if we have melted together into one. If this is what a kiss of his feels like, then I want everything, I want to feel every single touch, every single caress that he is willing to offer me.

Maybe I also feel this complete exhilaration because of the drugs I am being given, but I have never felt so alive. Whatever this is, I hope it continues. I don't know how long we kiss, but it feels like the ground is moving under my feet, like I am being lifted into the air.

"Well, it looks like you are both feeling better." Tal's amused words have my saviour raising his head. I want to scream at him not to stop, but instead I raise my hand to the one of his that is cupping my cheek and hold it there.

"Thank you, Brother."

His words have me frowning. What is he thanking Tal for?

"Nothing to it. I know you would have done the same for me, but next time you decide to go out and act like a hero, make sure you are wearing a helmet."

I smile when I realize that these two know each other quite well by the way they are bantering. Does that mean that Tal was taking care of me because he thought I belonged to his friend? The thought is sweet when I think of the lengths he went to for his friend.

"What happened to Haldor's sister?" my saviour suddenly asks.

I glance towards Tal, only to see his smiling expression change to one of sadness as he shakes his head.

"She didn't make it," he states.

"Shit! How is he?"

Tal shakes his head at the question. "You know

Haldor," he says, "he doesn't talk much, but he's one of the guys still on the ground looking for the staff."

"Who is with him?" my saviour asks, a scowl marring his face.

"Garth and Colborn have stayed behind to keep an eye on him. Beowulf, Zerek, and Vain from the Johannesburg chapter have also stayed," Tal updates as he places his arms on the back of the seat as he leans on it. Only now do I realize that the plane has taken off and we are now in the air. No wonder I felt like I was floating. I was literally in the air.

"Garth is going to have his hands full. Shit, if we hear that Qatar has burned to the ground we will know why. You couldn't have left a crazier bunch of motherfuckers behind."

I gasp. Is that where we were?

Immediately both men's eyes turn towards me.

"Are you in pain?" my saviour asks.

"No, I'm fine, I just realized for the first time where I was."

"It's you!" I am surprised to suddenly see a woman throwing herself at my saviour.

His hand pulls away from my cheek and my first reaction is to tear the woman away from him. I have never been a violent person, but I swear the drive is there and maybe it's a good thing that I still can't move that well because I am sure I would be doing it too.

The anger that fills me is surprising, as I feel a blinding jealousy—a blinding rage at seeing another woman in his arms. To his credit, he is pulling the woman away from him, lifting her to stand up.

"You are alive. I was so worried you had died."

"I am fine," he mutters in a completely different tone that he uses with me.

"Thank you. You saved me—you saved us." She is about to throw herself at him again, but Tal slips his arm around her waist, holding her back. He has just won my eternal gratitude with that action.

"Let's try not to kill him off just yet, Darling," he says smoothly as he takes a step back.

"Oh, oh of course. I'm so sorry," she says. "I don't know how you did what you did with that water, but I am in your debt."

"No need. I'm glad you are okay," he replies with a smile.

"Why don't I help you to your seat, you shouldn't be walking around," Tal says as he starts ushering her away.

"Looks like you're the real hero." I say, glad that he helped that woman, but also still angry that she jumped into his arms like that. How many women has he got jumping into his arms? "Do you have many women jumping into your arms like that?"

Damn, I didn't mean to blurt that out.

"No," he mutters, not at all reassuring.

"Why don't you rest, it's a long time still until we land," he says by placing his hand over mine on the arm rest of the seat. I might still be in a daze, but I know when someone is sidestepping from talking.

Huffing in irritation, I pull my hand from under his, placing it on my lap. But no sooner do I do that, he is lifting it again to where it was.

"Stop sulking."

I turn my head to look at him again, glaring in irritation. *How dare he tell me to stop sulking. Who does he think he is?* "I'm not sulking, and even if I was, it has nothing to do with you," I say angrily.

"That's where you are wrong. It has everything to do with me and you know it," he states.

"Really? And why is that? Just because you saved my life doesn't mean you own me," I snap in irritation, wondering how just a couple of minutes ago we were getting along so well, and now it has all derailed.

"Actually, baby girl, you are my mate, so I own every part of you."

What the hell is he talking about, or better yet, what has he been smoking?

"You are making no sense. That gash on your head must have affected you worse than you think," I state as I turn my head away from him and close my eyes. I won't give him the benefit of continuing this fight. I try to pull my hand away again. But it's to no avail because he tightens his hold on it.

Irritating, overbearing, and savage.

EIRIK 7

Sleep eludes me as I sit through the long flight watching Siena rest. My head is starting to feel better with each hour that passes, but my emotions are in turmoil. Her jealousy is a natural factor when it comes to mates. Yesterday, when I finally woke up from my unconsciousness and Tal started to provoke me about how he was enjoying spending time with Siena, I was ready to kill him, even though I knew that he was just provoking me. The thought of Siena enjoying any time at all with any other man has me seeing red.

That fact alone confuses me, as I was never possessive of Isabela. If men spoke to her or flirted with her it didn't bother me, but just the thought of any man looking at Siena has my berserker rearing its head, ready to kill.

She was angry at that woman throwing herself at me. How is she going to feel when she finds out that I married another woman? I don't regret the fact that I married Isabela; I don't regret the time I spent with her. She was a good, loving woman that gave me everything of herself. I close my eyes, leaning my head back as I think of the life I had before and how it has changed throughout the years.

I met Isabela in Italy; her family owned a little vineyard just outside of what is now Tuscany. For a short time, I thought that I could make a life there, that I could live a peaceful life among the humans that had taken me in, even though I was different. When Isabela died everything changed. I felt restless, so I brought her coffin to South Africa and buried her here among my brothers.

At the time it was just a handful of us, hiding from the world. We all have our crosses to bare, and even though we have fought together for many centuries, we have all in some way or another tried to live different lives.

I fought with Tor in many battles. We met when he was riding the seas looking for fortune as a Viking. Our bond solidified as we saved each other's lives countless times throughout the years. The others started to join us as we travelled through life. Tor already knew Draco because they had met a century before I met him. Draco and Tor go back a long time, so when Draco started the Elementals MC for all the men out there that are lost, and fighting to keep their sanity—fighting not to turn into Keres, we agreed to join. But Tor, being the alpha that he is, decided to take his own chapter in Cape Town.

It hasn't always been easy. We have lost men that

submitted to their darkness and had to be killed, or they themselves took their own lives rather than becoming the monsters our darkness brings out in us. This was before Draco found a way to keep the darkness back by helping us hold on to our light until we find our mates.

When I returned to South Africa with Isabela's coffin, it was Tor that kept me grounded. It was the fighting of evil—the fighting of darkness that kept me alive. Now that I have met my mate, I already feel a difference, a peace that I have never felt before, not even with Isabela. The fact that another woman has been able to touch me in a way that my wife never could makes me feel guilty. It feels like in some way I am betraying her memory.

I squeeze my eyes tightly, trying to shut out the anger building inside of me. The hopelessness at this situation, the hopelessness of disappointing yet another woman. Siena will hate the fact that I took another woman as my wife. She will not accept the fact that I loved another enough to marry her. I know that, because if Siena told me that she loved another man, I know I would lose my mind with rage.

Sighing, I open my eyes, turning my head I look at my woman sleeping peacefully next to me. I need to explain everything to Siena. I need to tell her what I am and that we are now mated. I know that after everything that has happened to her, this is the last thing I should be burdening her with, but I want her to know that no matter what she will be protected.

Sighing, I lift my hand to stroke her hair, then immediately drop it again. I need to get my head straight before I can be with Siena.

Einar is making his way towards us, his eyes on Siena's sleeping form. "How is she doing?" he asks as he comes to stand next to my seat.

"She seems better." At least she has some fire in her which last time she didn't.

"And you?" he asks with a raised brow.

"I'm healing. Will be good by the time we land."

"That wasn't what I was asking," Einar replies as he inclines his head towards Siena.

"It was unexpected, and it will be a change, but I will sort my shit out." I rub at the stubble on my jaw, frustrated with myself and the situation. I don't want to hurt Siena, and I know that her knowing about my relationship with Isabela will do that.

"In another couple of hours, we will be home, and then you will have lots of time to settle in," Einar says as he looks towards the end of the plane and nods to someone. "We will talk later; I still need to meet your woman." And with those words, he walks away towards the back, leaving me with my thoughts.

"What's your name?"

My eyes snap towards Siena. Because of my conversation with Einar, I didn't hear the change in her breathing announcing that she was waking.

"Eirik."

She frowns. "Is that your name?" At my nod she asks, "what does it mean?"

"Eternal ruler."

"And are you?"

Her question has my brows raising. "No, Tor is the one that rules our club in Cape Town." My answer has her turning her head towards the front. I see her wince, but she doesn't complain. "Are you in pain?"

"No, I just feel stiff," she confesses. "Do you know what they did to my back?"

"No, but when we get to the club Bion will come out to examine you."

"How long am I going to stay at the club?"

Her question has me stiffening. Does she have someone she wants to get back to? The thought has my anger rising.

"Why?" I snap, which has her head turning slightly towards me again.

"I want to phone my parent. I'm sure they will be worried about me and seeing as the club is in Cape Town, they can come and pick me up because they also live in Cape Town.

"You're not going anywhere." My answer has her face tensing, which reminds me about the ordeal she has just lived through. Telling her that she can't go somewhere will clearly not sit well with her. I quickly try to amend my reply as not to alarm her. "You are still in danger; they will know everything about you."

"Are my parents in danger?"

Her worried tone has me berating myself for making her unnecessarily upset.

"You can tell them to come and see you, they can come whenever they want for as long as they want." I'm sure the others won't love that, but they will understand. I see her visibly relax at my statement, her expression becoming less afraid.

"Are all the women staying there, too?"

I shake my head. "No, only you. The others will go to a compound that we have." When we first started healing the Elementals that were on the verge of turning into Keres, Draco organized a compound where Elementals and Keres that have been healed can stay for a time before going back to their chapters. This compound will now be used temporarily for the healing of the women.

Photos will be taken of each one and sent to all the clubs where the other brothers will see if any of them are their mates. I know by seeing Dag in action, that by simply seeing your mates' photo will ignite the recognition that is inbred in all of us of our mate.

Hopefully, some of the men will find their mates, and finally feel the peace that I am now feeling as I sit next to Siena. My passion might be driving me, but all the other emotions are stronger than I ever thought possible.

"Why am I staying at the club if all the other women aren't?"

"Because you are mine."

My statement has her eyes widening in surprise.

"Siena, I'm sure you can feel the connection between us."

Her expression doesn't change as she continues looking at me.

"When I first saw you, I realized that you were my mate. You see, this might sound really fucking crazy to you, but you know that the reason why all the women were taken was because you all have special gifts?"

"Yes, Tal said so, but how does that make me yours if you don't even know me?"

Stroking my thumb over the smooth skin of her inner wrist, I try to calm her as I hear her heart starting to race.

"All the Elemental men are different too,"

"Oh, that makes sense," she says, "of course there would also be men with certain abilities if there are women." Her statement has me shaking my head.

"I don't mean like that, true, we do have abilities but not like you think." Sitting forward I turn in my seat so that she can see me more clearly. This long flight can't be good for her back, if she weren't so heavily medicated, I am sure that she would be in pain. "As the name dictates, we are all able to bend a specific element."

"Like fire?"

Why is it that everyone always thinks of fire first? At my irritated thought, I shake my head.

"Yes, like fire, but my element is water."

"Does that mean you can find water, or that you can do things with water?" Before I can reply she continues, "what exactly can you do with water?"

It looks like my woman is a curious little thing.

"Yes, I can find water and yes I can do different things with it."

"I can conduct electricity."

Her proud statement has me smiling. It looks like she is competitive too. "Does that mean that I might electrocute you?"

Her sudden, horrified expression has my smile turning into a grin.

"No, you won't electrocute me. Why? Will you try?"

My question has her glaring at me. "Of course not, I'm not like that," she snaps.

"I know. I'm teasing you," I say, not wanting to rile her up. "But as I was saying, we are not like your normal man out there. Our abilities are more enhanced, and so is our strength, sight, and hearing."

"You are saying that you can hear and see better than most people?"

"What I am saying is that we aren't exactly human, and before you ask, I'm not an alien." My statement suddenly has a grin splitting across her face.

"That's a shame. Aliens sound pretty cool right now." Her joking has me growling playfully. I see she doesn't believe me and thinks that I am teasing her, but with time, she will understand that what I am saying is true.

"It's true, Siena, and as Elementals, we only have one mate. When we find that woman she will bring light into our life, and peace to our soul. You are that woman for me." My words have a giggle escape her lips.

"In my case, I will bring the electricity that you will need to get your own light bulb to light up your life," she quips with a laugh.

"I'm being serious, and with time, you will see that I am telling you the truth. Like it or not, you are mine." Those words are more intense than I wanted, but she needs to understand that she is mine and no matter what, we will work it out and make it work.

"I have a drop-dead handsome guy telling me I am

his. You think I'm going to complain?" she asks with a raised brow and a grin on her face. I can tell she still thinks I'm teasing her It's time to show her that she's mine, because it doesn't look like words are doing the trick.

Raising my hand, I slide it behind her neck, seeing her expression sombre immediately, as she sees me nearing. When our lips touch, it's a feeling like I have never had before, it's like coming home. It's at this moment that I decide that no matter what, Siena is my future and everything that happened in the past is the past.

Her murmur of pleasure has my cock straining against my zipper. I don't know when I will be able to make Siena fully mine as we still need to understand what was done to her back and try to help her. But I do know that she is mine and even if I haven't consummated our union yet, she will understand that. "You are mine!" I growl against her lips before deepening the kiss.

Doing this here is uncomfortable and crazy, but she is my woman, and it is time that she realizes what that means. I feel her hand against my heart, the warmth like a scorching poker reminding me of Isabela, which I promised to love for the rest of my life. I break the kiss abruptly, our hearts racing, and I realize that they are in rhythm with each other, beating to the same tune, to the same rhythm.

I'm sorry, Isabela!

SIENA 8

I have never been inside a motorcycle club, but if I had to imagine it, I would never get it right. Are all MCs like this one? When Eirik carries me in, the first thing I see is a bar area, which I expected, but what I didn't expect was the luscious black couches to one side, or the risqué décor.

As Eirik starts making his way inside, I see various men and some women that call out a greeting. Some of the men I have already seen when I was in Qatar, but there are three that are new to me and the women too. They seem friendly as I hear them talking. If I am going to be here for a long time, I would like to meet everyone, and hopefully I will be able to get up and start moving around soon. I am so tired of not being able to see the sun that if I could, I would sit outside the whole day, every day.

"We are going to Church soon; I will ask Anastasia to bring you some food," Eirik's comment surprises me. I never took him for someone that would go to church.

"I didn't take you for the religious type."

My statement has him stopping. A stunned look on

his face that quickly transforms into a grin.

"Umm, when I say Church, I mean a meeting."

Oh, I feel my cheeks heat with embarrassment. I should have kept my mouth shut. It's the first time he has smiled since he kissed me earlier on the plane. One minute, he was blowing my mind with passion, the next he is getting up and saying he has to talk to someone. He was gone until just before we landed.

One minute he is running hot, the next he is freezing cold. I don't know what to do with him, and that story he was telling me. I'm sure he must have been teasing me, but he seemed so sincere that I am confused and unsure of what to believe.

I do know that if it was true, I wouldn't look back. Eirik touches me in a way that no one else ever has, and I don't mean only passionately. Even though he makes me forget everything and everyone when he touches me, I mean emotionally and mentally as well.

Eirik ignites my senses—my mind in a way that I'm not used to. I seem to have a connection with him even though I have only known him for such a short time. I do know that there is a kind of connection between us that is palpable, and if that story he told me is true, then I am going to jump in with both feet.

I thought for sure that I was going to die if I didn't leave that place and thought that I would never have a normal life again. And even though I doubt I will ever be able to have children, not with all the experiments they did on me, at least I can have a man that wants me, that cares for me, and that will make a home for me.

Glancing up, I admire Eirik as he approaches his bedroom. His strong jaw has a few days of stubble that instead of making him look scruffy, gives him a rebellious look that only enhances his manly features.

Eirik stops to open the door. Even though I now have more movement, I still get frustrated because everything still seems to be going in slow motion.

He walks towards the bed, sitting me on the mattress carefully before moving to fix the pillows against the impressive oak headboard of the bed. My eyes lift to the painting of the woman above the bed, her long silky brown hair and pouty red lips talking of passion. Her eyes filled with laughter and maybe even love. She is a beautiful woman; her corset seems to be from another era.

Eirik lifts me again, pulling me up against the headboard and the pillows. His bed is comfortable, something I haven't had in a very long time as the men had makeshift beds put up for all the women. "Who's the woman?" I ask, curious to why he would have a painting of a woman above his bed.

Is she his mother? That would just be creepy. His head snaps up and I see him stiffen as he looks at the painting. "I have to go; we will talk when I get back," he mutters as he makes his way towards the door and leaves.

"What the hell?" I whisper as he does it again. I try to look and bend my neck back so I can look up at the painting, but I am still too stiff to manage much. "Darn," I snap

"Well, that doesn't sound promising!"

I gasp at her words as I look towards the door. Because Eirik left in such a hurry, he forgot to close the door. Which is the reason why I didn't hear the woman come in. She is one of the women that were in the bar area, a friendly smile on her face as she looks at me. She must be Anastasia that Eirik mentioned.

"Sorry to startle you. I am Freya."

Maybe not. I guess Anastasia is one of the others.

"Hi, I'm Siena. Sorry about that I'm still stiff and can't move as I would like."

"Do you need any help? Anastasia will be coming soon with something for you to eat, and I'm sure Esmeralda will pop in soon too." Well, it looks like I will be getting more visitors than I thought.

"For now I'm fine, thank you."

Freya walks towards me, taking a seat by my feet as she looks at me. Oh, my word, it can't be?

"I know you," I mutter, "or I think it's you."

She grins at my surprise.

"You're an actress, aren't you?"

"Yes, but I'm a *former* actress," she says with a wink.

"Do you live here?"

"Yes. Dane is my mate." There is that word again. "You will meet him later. I will bring him here so you can meet. They had to go into a meeting to catch up on everything, but it shouldn't take too long."

Before I can ask her about why she calls Dane her mate, another woman walks in with a plate in hand. This must be Anastasia.

"Hi, I believe you must be hungry after such a long flight."

"Yes, I find as time passes, my appetite grows too. I am starving."

She smiles as she places the tray on my lap.

"Ulrich told me you were kidnapped. I'm so sorry," Anastasia says.

"Ulrich is her mate," Freya interrupts.

"Why do you call them mates?"

Now that I got the opportunity again, I am not going to waste it. But I see that my question has both women looking at each other in surprise.

"Hasn't Eirik told you about the Elementals?" Anastasia asks.

"That they are different? Yes, but are they?"

My question has both women suddenly grinning.

"So, you don't believe him?" Freya asks.

"Well, he said they're not human." I roll my eyes for emphasis, but I see both women don't seem surprised.

"It's true," Freya replies,

"So, the whole 'you're my mate' speech is true?" Why would these women confirm his story if it wasn't true?

"Yes, it is," Anastasia confirms. "Ulrich is mine, Dane is Freya's and Dag is Esmeralda's."

"He said that elementals only have one mate and that I am his. Does that mean that he has never… umm… you know?" My question has both women burst out laughing.

"Oh, I wish, wouldn't that be something?" Anastasia replies with a grin.

"If you are asking if they sleep around, oh yeah. And to be fair, with all the years they have lived to have to wait for their mate would be a crime, but the moment they find us then that is it." She shrugs at that. "They are completely and utterly committed, even if they wanted to it wouldn't work with anyone else." She winks when saying that.

"Are you serious?"

They both nod at my question.

"You said all the years they have lived, how old are they?"

"Well, I think Eirik is one of the oldest here, after Tor, that is. He would be five or six hundred years old."

She must be joking.

"Hi, sorry I'm late." My eyes raise to look at the woman standing in the doorway. This must be Esmeralda, and if I remember correctly, Dag's mate. This is crazy. I can't believe that I am actually taking them seriously.

"Esmeralda, come meet Siena," Anastasia calls, and I see when she approaches that she must be in her early stages of pregnancy. Does that mean that they can have children?

"We were just updating Siena on our guys," Freya says. "Why don't you take a seat next to her and relax."

This has Esmeralda sigh, and by the scowl on her face I would say in irritation.

"If I rest anymore, I will never move again," she mumbles as she takes the seat next to me on the bed.

The other two women grin.

"Don't mind her. Dag is driving her crazy," Anastasia says as she leans forward and strokes Esmeralda's baby bump.

"I wish it was only Dag. Did you know that Einar just offered to carry me here?" she says in irritation.

"I swear I'm going to skip town and only come back when this kid is born."

"You want to kill your man of heart failure?" Freya asks jokingly, then looking at me she continues, "One thing you can expect from the men is that they are overprotective. If your mate isn't around then the others will make sure to keep you safe." That has me thinking back to Tal and the way he kept on asking if I was fine and making sure that I had everything that I needed.

"Do you know who this woman above the bed is?" I see the three women look up at the painting and then at each other, which immediately has my jealousy rising. There is something about this woman, I just know there is.

"Well, umm…" Anastasia starts looking uncomfortable. "I'm not sure about the whole story, so you might have to ask Eirik for the details, but I believe that her name was Isabela, and she was his wife."

"What?" To say that I am shocked is an understatement, and here I was starting to believe everything they were telling me about this whole mate thing. "I thought you said that they only mated once."

"They do, that's why I say that you need to ask

Eirik about all the details," Anastasia replies. "What I know is that he married her a couple of hundred years ago, but she died."

"If she wasn't his mate, then it doesn't make sense that he married her, now does it?" I feel so hurt at the fact that he was married, and I don't even know why. The thought that he loved that woman is blinding, and of course he loved her, or he wouldn't still have her painting hanging above his bed. If he thinks that I am going to be with him as a substitute just because he can't actually have the one he loves, then he has chosen the wrong woman.

"I'm not going to stay in this room," I state, which has all three-women looking surprised.

"Maybe let him explain before you decide. Maybe it's not what you think," Freya says with a worried look on her face.

"You say he married her hundreds of years ago, and still he has a painting of her above his bed. What does that tell you?"

"She could take Garth's room; he won't mind, as he's still in Qatar," Esmeralda suggests.

I met Garth while in Qatar and even though he just greeted me as he spoke to Tal, he didn't seem like the type that might be upset by me using his bed while he's away.

"Eirik's not going to like it," Anastasia says.

"I don't care what he likes, he might have saved me, but he doesn't tell me what to do." I sound more confident than I feel, but I will not be sharing Eirik with a memory of a dead wife.

"Can you walk there?" Freya asks as she looks me up and down. Something which I didn't think about clearly.

"I will try." Even If I have to crawl there but I won't stay here with this painting hanging over my head.

"Where are you hurt, what happened?" Esmeralda asks as she places a hand over my hand, looking over at her I get the feeling that this woman isn't a stranger to pain, and by placing her hand on mine she understands the horrors that I lived.

"They were experimenting on us. Just before Eirik found me they did something to my back which I am still recuperating from. Eirik says that Bion will come and examine me now that I am here, but it's really frustrating, because to move it's in slow motion as you see, and I can't even see what they have done."

"Would you like me to have a look and tell you?"

Esmeralda asks, her eyes kind.

"Sure, but I will have to move forward first before you can see anything." Just the thought is daunting when I think about needing to shuffle forward for her to be able to pick up the loose T-shirt that someone got for me to wear when I was in Qatar to look at my back.

"We will help," Anastasia says as she comes around the bed to stand next to me. "Scream if we hurt you."

"Trust me, I will." I meant it as a joke, but I do think that I would scream if jolted. Anastasia places her hands under my arms, Freya slides her arms around my waist, her face flush with my side.

"Okay slowly, lets pull her forward," Freya says.

"Ahhh," I whimper as they pull, which has them stopping immediately.

"Nope, I don't think this is a good idea," Freya says in a concerned voice.

"Are you okay?" Esmeralda asks, a horrified look on her face. Am I? There is a slight pain which I didn't have before, but otherwise it seems fine.

"Yes, I think its fine, but I don't think I should try to move like that." I start moving my leg to the side, it's tiring but I'm able. "Maybe if I do it like this."

"Sweetheart, not to be funny, but tonight you will still be trying to move off this bed at this speed," Anastasia says as she starts to walk towards the door. "I'm going to get a prospect."

EIRIK 9

"I'm glad to see you guys are back in one peace, even though I heard you nearly lost your head," Ulrich quips as I walk in. He is already sitting at his place, Dag next to him.

"Depends how you look at it. Some would say he has," Tal teases as he comes up behind me.

"Yeah, I heard you found your mate." Dag says as he looks up from his phone at me.

"She's a sweet little thing, way too sweet for the likes of him," Tal replies with a laugh, but I'm not in a teasing mood. My thoughts are on Siena and her question just before I left. What the fuck am I going to say to her? I completely forgot about Isabela's painting; I have had it there for so long that most of the time I don't even realize that it's there anymore.

I will have to bring it down; I feel guilty at the thought of getting rid of something that Isabela gave me with so much love, but I know that it's not fair to Siena to have it up in our bedroom.

"Earth to, Eirik, anyone there?" I look towards Tal

to see him looking at me with a raised brow. "You, okay? You haven't heard a thing we have said." I realize that the others are also looking at me. I am saved from answering as Tor, Dane, and Einar walk in and take their places.

"Let's try to make this short," Tor grunts as he leans back in his chair. "We got confirmation that Aldor is somewhere in Mexico. Celmund has open access to Zorba International network, he penetrated their system and found various plans for new warehouses around the world, but there is nothing about the experiments they are doing."

"There must be something, somewhere," Ulrich says as he places his arms on the table and looks around at everyone.

"Bro, you should have seen that place," Tal reiterates. "They are organized. All the women were separated into different buildings. You can see that they are meticulous."

"Yes, that is true," Tor agrees. "I have just spoken to Garth, and he says that they have only found two of the doctors that worked there, and that was just because they were lucky as they were already on their way out of the country."

"Yeah, the fuckers had everything rigged." Einar looks towards Ulrich, Dane and Dag, that weren't with us in Qatar. "If it wasn't for Katrina, Draco's woman contacting him to let him know that one of the other women in his chapter had a vision of bombs in the buildings, we would have had some of our men killed instead of just a bump on Eirik's head." They all look at me, but even though the top of my head is still tender, I have taken the bandage off and am looking normal.

"How's the head?" Tor asks with a raised brow.

"Tender but getting better."

"Did we get any information on how they are using the women to enhance those guys?"

"Everything we got has gone to Natura Valley Chapter, Celmund and Bion will look through everything and try to make sense of what they are up to," Tor updates as he raises his hand to slide his fingers around the back of his neck and massage there.

"So, what do we do while they are doing that? Are we just going to sit around?" I ask angrily. After what I saw in Qatar and after what they did to Siena, I want the fuckers stopped.

"We are getting information on the other buildings the Zorba own, but in the meantime, we do have a war going on here if you have forgotten," Tor snaps, after everything we saw in Qatar and the long days of trying to get as much information as possible before leaving and coming home, we are all running on short fuses.

"Yeah, Basil tried to blow Dane up when he went into Town yesterday." My eyes snap to Dane. But he seems fine.

"What happened?" I ask. We should just obliterate those fuckers once and for all.

"Was when I went to collect all of Dag's toys." Dane replies sarcastically.

"Don't blame that shit on me, you were also picking up stuff for yourself." Dag replies

"Yeah, one packet. You fucking bought the whole store. Where are you going to put all that stuff?" Dane asks sarcastically.

"I just bought what they say a child should have," Dag mutters grumpily.

"What about those boob hubcaps?" Dane asks and then looks at us. "Did you know that women wear hubcaps on their boobs?"

"What the fuck are you talking about?" Tor asks.

"I swear Tor, those things look like hub caps and

this fucker had me go and pick them up," Dane grumbles, shaking his head.

"They're not hub caps for fuck's sake, they are nipple protectors for when women breastfeed," Dag replies angrily.

"You are shitting me!" Tal says with a laugh. "Dag, what the hell dude."

"What? It says that it's important…"

"Enough!" Tor roars. "I don't want to fucking hear about that shit. You guys can talk all about woman's hubcaps when we're done." He turns towards me, his eyes stormy with pent up anger. "How's your woman doing?"

"She seems to be moving easier. They did something to her back, but Bion said that he would come and see her here and figure out how we can fix it."

"Yeah, they did a number on her. I still can't understand what that piece of steel is doing there."

My eyes snap to his. What the fuck does he mean by a piece of steel?

"What piece of steel?"

"You haven't seen it?" he asks, surprised.

"If you haven't noticed, I was unconscious for most of our stay in Qatar. How was I supposed to have seen it when I wasn't with Siena?"

"Shit, Brother, I thought you had seen what they did to her back." Tal leans forward, a scowl now on his face. "There is a round piece of steel, looks kind of like the mechanisms of a watch attached to her spine."

Hearing that has my inner darkness rising with fury, how dare they do something like that?

"Bion had a look before he left. He was worried that it could be explosive because apparently the Keres were doing that to some women a few years back, but it's not." He raises his hand to his jaw, rubbing it as if to ease the tenseness there. "That's how I saw it."

"Sons of bitches," Ulrich growls. "Coming from Keres it's understandable as they are evil through and through, but weren't the damn doctors human? How can humans do that to other humans?"

"In the name of science," Tor states with a shrug. "That's always their excuse."

"If we have only found two of the doctors that worked there, and the five that were in the buildings at the time we attacked, do we know how many more there are?" Einar asks.

Tor sits forward as he gives us an update. "No, Haldor killed the two before they could be questioned, and from the five, they're not talking, so, Draco is having Aria listening to the questioning." Aria is Brandr's mate and a mind reader. She is our secret weapon when we need information and it's quite uncomfortable when she's around because we never know if she is listening to what we are thinking.

"For now, we forget about Qatar until we have more information. I want us to go out there and let the gangs see us," Tor orders. "Dane, do you know which of the gangs rigged your cage?"

The Desperados have joined forces with other gangs to try to conquer this war we have going. But what they don't know is that this war was won even before it started. We could have killed every single one of them if we wanted to, but instead we let them breathe, hoping that they would lead us to the bigger fish. Now that we know who the big fish is, we don't need the gangs any longer and can end this irritating squabble.

"Yeah, I saw them as they hurried away," Dane replies.

"Lucky for you or you would be in pieces," Tal

states.

"Yeah, don't think Freya would be pleased with me if that happened."

"I want you all to keep your eyes peeled, and no going out alone" Tor looks pointedly at Dane as he speaks. I'm sure he has already given him a lashing as we were told as soon as the war started that no one rides alone. "Eirik, I want you to stay behind. The rest of you can go."

Shit, what now? I'm not in a hurry to get back to my room as I still haven't thought about what I am going to tell Siena, but I'm also not in the mood to talk strategies right now. When everyone leaves, Tor stands and leans on the table, his arms crossing as he looks down at me. "How's your head with everything that has happened?" I know that he's not asking about the accident I had, and even though I wish we wouldn't talk about this, I owe him this.

Tor has always been there when I needed help. He was the one that was there when Isabela died, and I brought her here to be buried. He gave me a purpose. And even though Isabela wasn't my mate, I felt lost when she died.

Now if I think about anything happening to Siena, I know nothing would appease me—nothing would calm my darkness except death. This metal piece she has attached to her spine came as a surprise to me, but I will do everything I can to help her. "It's fine," I reply.

Tor tenses. "Don't fucking play games with me. I know you."

I sigh, feeling the rage in Tor's eyes. I stand because I am too wound up to sit here around doing nothing. I start to pace to try to rid myself of some of the excess energy I feel.

"I find out I have a mate, and then I'm surprised by the fact that she has a fucking metal piece attached to her spine which we still don't know what it is." The anger I am feeling is evident in my voice, but I know Tor will expect nothing less from me. "Then I come home to try to make her comfortable and start a life with a woman that I didn't even know I wanted, only to forget Isabela's painting is still hanging in my fucking room."

"Shit," Tor mutters.

"You don't say," I reply sarcastically.

"What did she say?"

"She asked me who it was."

"And?"

"I told her we would talk after this meeting." Lifting both my hands, I rub at my face, feeling the tension pulling at my neck.

"What are you going to tell her?"

"Whatever I tell her isn't going to go down well, is it?" I ask, when I finally stop to look at him.

Tor shakes his head as he stands up straight. He uncrosses his arms as he walks towards me. "All I know is that I have seen some crazy situations when it comes to mates, and one thing I have learnt is that no matter what, you guys will sort it out." He places his hand on my shoulder. "She's your mate, Brother, that means that she will understand you."

"Or electrocute me," I quip.

"What do you mean?" Tor asks with a frown.

"She can manipulate electricity, that's her gift."

A grin spreads across Tor's face. "Yeah, wait until I tell Draco. That's a great gift to have at our club." I shake my head at his competitiveness. Ever since Ulrich mated, Tor has been excited with the fact that we will have our own women army, like the Natura Valley chapter has. He doesn't like the fact that he has to curb his eccentric behaviour when the women are around, but he likes the fact that each woman has her own special gift that can be used to help us if ever needed.

"You won't be saying that if they start taking over your club like the women do in his chapter."

My comment has him tensing, and he grunts. "Curb your tongue, Eirik, that won't happen here," he states.

"We shall see. Wait until you find your woman."

"She will do as I say!"

His forceful words have me shaking my head. Let's hope that's true because otherwise, I am going on holiday while they sort it out, because Tor can be a real pain when he's upset. We both turn towards the door when we hear approaching footsteps. "Dag," Tor states as we sense Dag's energy approaching.

"Celmund is on the line," Dag says as he opens the door.

"Coming." Tor heads for the door, but before he steps out, he glances back. "For what it's worth, I'm glad you found your woman, Brother, you need her."

I know Tor was worried about me above everyone else here at the club, because he knew that I wasn't expecting to find my mate and instead was prepared to die.

Taking a deep breath, I head towards the door. It's time I face my problems. Making my way to the room, I tense as I open the door and then freeze. Where the fuck is Siena? I head towards the bathroom, only to stop when I see it empty.

"Of course, she's not here," I mutter to myself. It's not as if she can move. The thought that some other man touched her has my anger bubbling. Closing my eyes, I feel the energy around me immediately, sensing my woman close. Exhaling in relief, I am about to go after her when I remember the fucking painting. Walking towards the bed, I lean over it and gently pull the painting away from the wall and off its hook. I will have to get this packed away somewhere, but for now I will slide it under the bed and then move it when I find a place to stash it. I make my way towards where I sense her, only to stop stunned, outside Garth's room.

Why is she in Garth's room? Everything in me rebels at the thought that my woman is in another man's bed that isn't mine. Turning the handle, I throw the door open, hearing it crash against the wall with a loud bang. Siena, who is reclining against the pillows in the centre of his bed, gasps in surprise. A look of shock is on her face as she stares at me.

"Ohh, what are you doing?"

I narrow my eyes. "What am I doing?" The anger coursing through my body has the words fighting to come out. My low tones warn anyone in the vicinity that I'm ready to wrench someone apart. "No, the question is what are you doing in Garth's bed?"

"I'm not staying in your room." Her stubborn lift of her chin has me wanting to shake her.

"You are not staying in here," I roar. It's a good thing that Garth isn't here because I would kill him even though this wasn't his doing. The thought of my woman in his bed where he has been laying has every type of scene flashing through my mind, driving me crazy.

Walking towards the bed, I slide my arm under her legs and the other behind her back. "No!" she snaps, but I continue to lift her, only to feel a tingling feeling race through my body.

"Are you trying to shock me?" I ask in surprise.

"Why isn't it working?" She must be powerful because for some reason, our women's gifts never work against us, but even in her weakened state, I can feel a tingle.

"Because you can't use your gift against elementals," I reply angrily, turning to make my way towards my room. "Who brought you in here?"

I'm going to skin the asshole that thought he could put his hands on my woman.

When she doesn't answer, I look down to see her glaring at me, her lips tightly shut. Grunting, I look back up as I walk into my room, banging it closed with the heel of my boot. "This is now your room, you stay here."

"No."

"Why not?" I snap, angry that she doesn't want to stay with me in the room.

"I'm not going to stay in the same room where you hold a shrine to your wife."

Shit, who the fuck told her?

"There is no shrine!" She gets me so fucking angry.

"I'm not going to sleep in a bed where you will be looking up at your dead wife while I'm in there," she reiterates. "So much for the one mate theory." With those words I can hear the hurt underneath her anger and it tears me apart. The last thing I want to do is hurt her. I promised myself I would never hurt another woman again, never make a woman suffer emotionally because of me again.

"I took it down, look!" I turn slightly so she can look at the wall, her head turns, and I see her looking at the place where the painting was. Now there's only a mark from it being against the wall for so many years.

"No painting but the mark is there to remind you of what was there." She says stubbornly.

"For Pete's sake, I'll paint the damn wall. Will that help?" Instead of answering, she huffs. Shaking my head, I walk towards the bed, placing her against the pillows that are still arranged against the headboard from earlier when she was here. I need to make sure to get the damn painting from under the bed and into storage before she finds out where it is, or she will most probably burn the damn thing to a crisp.

My woman is a lit firecracker when she's upset!

SIENA 10

"Bion has arrived."

Looking up from my chair near the window, I smile at Esmeralda that is sitting opposite me. Her senses are more in tune with everything around her, more than most people. Therefore, she can hear, sense, feel and see better than anyone else, even more than the Elementals. From what I have heard, theirs are also quite enhanced. This last week since arriving at the club has been a rollercoaster, but luckily, I'm starting to get my movement back and can already stand and walk even though it's really slow.

Today, Bion has come to see me, something Eirik mentioned this morning before he disappeared. Ever since our argument I have hardly seen him. If it wasn't for the women keeping me company, I would be as alone here as I was when I was captured.

I know that he sleeps with me at night because sometimes his side of the bed is still warm, and only today was he still in the room when I woke up, but I think that is because he wanted to tell me that Bion was coming. When I saw him this morning all I wanted to do was for him to kiss me, for him to show me what it's like to be his mate, but he doesn't seem to want to even be in the same room as me.

"I hope he can figure out a way to take that thing out of my back." Anastasia took a photo of my back and I finally was able to see what was done. I was horrified at the long scar running the length of my back, but what horrified me the most was the round metal dial right in the middle of my back, as if I was a robot. I'm worried that if it is taken off, then I won't be able to move again, depending on what they have done.

But the women swear by Bion's abilities as a healer, and apparently his mate Brielle has a gift of healing as well. But Brielle is also pregnant and won't be coming with Bion today. "Has Bion been the one to give you a check-up once you found out you were pregnant?" Even though I met Bion before, I am nervous of what he will say once he has a chance to see exactly what they have done to my back.

"Yes, and he is great," Esmeralda replies as she lowers her kindle. "I never thought I could become pregnant, so you can understand that I had no idea the reason I wasn't feeling well was because I was pregnant." She shrugs with a smile. "To be honest, I was convinced that I didn't want children. I didn't want to bring an innocent life into this world full of treacheries." She slides her hand over her stomach lovingly. "But then I felt him move and everything changed."

"You know it's a boy?"

"No, but Dag and I are hoping for a boy," she confesses with a smile.

"Well, hello, ladies." I turn my head to see Bion standing in the doorway with Eirik right behind him.

"Hi, Bion, I haven't seen you in a while," Esmeralda calls.

"Yeah, a lot has been happening lately. How are you feeling, darling?" He isn't just a good healer, he seems to be great with his patients too.

"I would be better if everyone stopped coddling me," she replies with a shrug. Bion comes to stand next to her, his head inclined, giving me the impression that he is listening to something.

"Would you like me to have a word with Dag?"

"Would you?" she asks with a happy expression.

"Leave it up to me," he promises with a teasing smile His head turns, and his eyes connect with mine. "What about you, sweetheart?"

"Don't know. I'm waiting for you to tell me," I say with a smile. Since I met him, he has been nothing but good to me.

"Well then, shall I start with some questions just to understand how you are feeling before we continue?"

"Of course."

"Well, that's my cue to leave," Esmeralda says as she stands to make her way out of the room. When Esmeralda leaves Eirik closes the door behind her and then leans against it, giving me the impression that he wants to stand as far away from me as possible, but still be able to see and know what Bion is doing.

"You can also leave. I'm fine with Bion."

My statement has his relaxed expression tensing and a scowl covering his face.

"No."

I huff at his stubbornness, but look at Bion, waiting for him to continue.

"I see you are moving more than when I first saw you. Are you still taking the painkillers?"

"I only take one in the morning," I reply. I can feel Eirik's eyes boring into me from where he's standing.

"That's good, and do you have pain?"

"Yes, every time I move." I would rather have the pain than be in limbo. After living through hell like I have in the last months, the pain I feel now when I move is bearable.

"Then why the fuck don't you take the pills?" Eirik suddenly asks, surprising me when I see him standing right next to me. "I will not have you in pain." His angry words have me tensing in anger.

How dare he! It's my body. I will treat it as I please.

"Please continue," I say sweetly to Bion, pointedly ignoring Eirik.

"Explain the pain to me. Is it centralized only to your back or does it shoot across your body when you move?" Bion too ignores the interruption as he continues with his questioning.

"It comes from my back to whichever body part I'm moving, but I am less stiff now." I can't wait to be moving around again with no stiffness and no pain. Hopefully, that will be possible in the future, because living like this after I have always been an active person is depressing.

"That is good," Bion says as he points. "Can I have a look at your back now?"

"You will have to help me pull the T-shirt off Sorry but one of the others still help me slip them on."

I see Bion looking at Eirik, his eyes moving behind me. This tells me that Eirik is now behind me. When I feel his fingers gently pull up the back of my T-shirt, I close my eyes. Feeling the warmth of his skin touching mine warms me.

I hear what sounds like a growl emitting from him when my T-shirt is bunched at the top of my shoulders. Only now remembering that he has never actually seen what they have done to my back. He definitely won't want anything to do with me now. How do I compare to his precious wife?

"Motherfuckers!" The word is expelled with such rage that I feel tears filling my eyes.

Bion moves behind me, and then I feel fingers gently prodding the area on my back, gasping when he touches an especially sensitive place. The growl comes again from Eirik, but this time louder. "Don't fucking hurt her!" His words are filled with anger—an anger for what was done to me—an anger for the pain that I am feeling.

Eirik does care if I'm in pain or not, that's why he

was upset that I'm not taking the painkillers. "Well, the good news is that this mechanism they have placed on your back has been imputed into five other women that I have already seen since Qatar. I wasn't sure if it was the same, but it seems like it is. Therefore, I will be able to extract it, and if it's anything like the others, you should be moving around with no pain in no time and back to normal in a month or so."

His words are like a ray of sunshine. I'm going to be fine. I will be able to do everything I did before. "When can you take it out?" I ask, wanting this thing out of me as soon as possible.

"In about an hour or so, if you are okay with that?"

"Yes, definitely."

"I'm going to have to put you to sleep to extract the item, but it shouldn't take too long," he explains as he comes to stand once again before me.

"Do you know what it does?" I have been curious to know what the purpose of this little piece of metal is on my back.

"I've been told that your gift is conducting electricity. The other women that had the same done to them also had similar gifts. I'm thinking that they were measuring the pulsations running through your body to try to replicate it." All this because of what I can do. "What they don't know is that we have found that women's gifts become more powerful when they mate. The same as us Elementals."

"Is it true that I can't electrocute the Elementals?" I don't want to ever hurt anyone unconsciously, and knowing that they are somehow immune to it will calm my mind.

Bion suddenly grins as his eyes raise to where Eirik is standing behind me. He has now pulled down my T-shirt, but his hands are on my shoulders, possessively.

"Wanting to electrocute anyone I know?" he asks with a wink, which has me smiling as I think that just a few days ago I did try to shock Eirik. "But it's true, your gift won't work on us." The way he says it makes me think that there is a possibility that it could, though, but he's reluctant to tell me.

"What about the women? They aren't elementals?"

He shakes his head. "When we bond and share blood with our women, their DNA transforms enough to protect them against most gifts, but if I were you, I wouldn't go out and try it, as it might just give someone a new hairstyle."

What does he mean by share blood? Eirik and I

didn't share blood. Does that mean that we are in fact not bonded? "Well, if there are no more questions, I will go prepare an area where I can do this procedure." He looks at Eirik. "You okay with this?"

Why is he asking him?

"Is there any danger to her having it removed?" Good question, I never thought about that.

"Not if it's like the others, which by appearance it seems to be."

"I will bring her through when it's time," Eirik's reply has Bion nodding before he turns and takes his leave.

"I thought you said I was your mate?" I ask the minute Bion is out the door and Eirik is standing before me.

"You are!"

"Okay. So we are mates, but we're not bonded?"

His eyebrow rises in question. "What are you trying to get at?" he asks as he folds his arms across his chest.

"Bion said that once blood is shared that our DNA changes, and we are bonded, but we haven't shared any blood, so that means that we aren't bonded."

"We did share blood. When I first took you from that place, you were unconscious, and I knew that my blood would help you heal faster." His confession has me gasping in surprise. How did I not know that? "So whatever ideas you have of us not being bonded, you can forget them. You are mine." His words are forceful and angry as he glares at me, but he doesn't know is that it's completely the opposite of what I want.

I do want to be Eirik's mate. I want that family life I always dreamed of. But my worry is that he doesn't want that, that he is still hung up on his dead wife. How can I ever compete with that? How can I ever compete with a memory?

"It's not as if you want this, is it?" I mutter once I see that he is halfway to the door.

My words have him stopping and slowly turning, his eyes flashing with anger. "Is it?" he growls before leaving with his back tense as he walks out of the room and down the corridor. I watch him until he turns, an imposing figure to anyone that wants to stand in his way. What kind of answer was that?

EIRIK 11

She is the most argumentative woman I have ever met. She knows just how to ignite my anger. Walking outside, I lift my helmet from the handlebars of my Harley and slide it on. I need to get out of here and get some space from Siena even if it's just for half an hour, because if not, I will explode.

Not being able to make her completely mine is driving me crazy. Every waking minute I'm tortured with images of what I want to do to her. Every night is pure torture lying next to her and not being able to show her how much I want her.

I never thought I could want someone as much as I want Siena, that I would care about someone as much as I care about her. Seeing what they did to her back is like a wrenching wound inside of me. I hate the fact that she's in pain and that I can't do anything to help her.

My bike roars to life, the sound vibrating through my body like the beat of my heart. Tor is going to be livid that I left alone, but I couldn't give a fuck. I need this before I have to touch Siena again, before she needs to go through another ordeal, all because she's different.

As I approach, the prospect opens the gate and I am flying out and down the road like a bat out of hell. The light drizzle is a balm to my overheated emotions—to my rebellious mind. I have made peace with the fact that I found my mate after thinking for centuries that fate had made a mistake by not making Isabela my mate.

I realize now the difference between a true bond and what I had with Isabela. The feelings I hold for Siena are a hundred-fold more intense than anything I ever felt for Isabela. I never thought this would be possible, that feelings like this were true, but she is like a fever in my blood.

I know that this must all be confusing for her, knowing that I had a wife when she has been told that we are mates won't make sense to her. Now that I have met Siena, I know my mistake, and even though I don't regret knowing Isabela, I regret that I hurt Siena because of it. I hope that one day she will understand.

She is excited about the fact that Bion is going to fix her back, but all I can think about is that he is going to cut into her again. What if it isn't the same as the other women's? What if there are complications? My heart is racing at the thought. I will lose my shit if anything happens to her.

I might only have known Siena for a couple of days, but I've been keeping an eye on her, and to see how she smiles at the women makes me want to be the one she smiles at. Her happy disposition, even though she's in pain, has made the others laugh.

The other women have been great, helping her in whatever is needed—being her real friends. I told Anastasia that if Siena wanted to call her parents, she should let her use her phone until I got Siena one, but Anastasia revealed that Siena only wanted to phone her parents once she knew what was happening with her back.

I open my throttle, letting the speed drive away my thoughts, and the wind and rain wash away my frustration. I need to show my woman that I want her, that I want only her, but how the fuck am I going to do that?

I'm not a soft man. I'm not a man that is known for my happy disposition. Instead, I am known for the anger that drives me, for my quick actions in a difficult situation. I am not known for my romantic poetry or glib tongue.

Racing around a bend, I suddenly come face to face with a truck across the road that has skidded and came to a holt. I brake, feeling my back tire start to skid but I hold it firm. The wet ground isn't helping the situation, and then a puddle on a slight dip is the tipping factor, bringing my bike down with a hard thwack.

The air is knocked out of me as I slide on the tarmac, stopping a foot away from the side of the overturned truck. I lay here for a few minutes, regaining my breath before I turn and slowly stand. "Shit," I mutter as I look down at my kutte, that is now scuffed from sliding on the tarmac.

My side is aching like a motherfucker, but I make my way towards my bike. Grabbing the handlebars and the back of my seat, I righten the bike placing it on its side stand. The tank's not looking too bad, just minor scratches, but the handlebars, footrests and exhaust took the brunt of it and will definitely need replacing. "It's not too bad, girl," I whisper. At least it will get me back home.

Turning, I head towards the truck, hearing voices on the other side. Coming around the back, I see that a car has pulled up, and what looks like the driver bent at the waist as he takes in deep breaths. Looks like everything is under control here. Time to get my ass back to the club and Siena, as it is time to get her fixed.

Fuck, my side is aching where I hit the ground. My jeans are torn down my leg, but luckily all the scratches will be better by tomorrow. The ride back to the club is slower than the one out, but when I finally park, I breathe out in relief. The Harley is sounding rough. Something got messed up in the fall.

"What the hell happened to you?" Dane asks, looking as if he was on his way out somewhere.

"There's a truck overturned at the junction near the exit to the highway, saw it too late to brake." He looks behind me and then down at my bike.

"Were you by yourself?"

"Yeah."

He shakes his head as he makes his way towards his bike just as Ulrich walks towards us from the workshop.

"Oh man, what did you do to your bike?" he asks, coming to squat down next to the bike to see its damage.

"Thanks, I'm fine," I say sarcastically.

"I can see that," he replies, which has me shaking my head as I make my way inside, leaving him to check out the bike.

"Well, looks like you saw your ass," Einar states, as

I walk past him to my room.

"Yeah, and it wasn't pretty," I mutter as I open the door and enter.

"Is he re..." Siena starts to ask, only to stop when she sees the state I'm in. "Oh, what happened? Are you hurt?" she starts to make her way towards me. I see the wince on her face as she takes a step which has me walk up to her.

"I'm fine, just wanted to see how hard the tar actually is," I quip, trying to make light of the situation, tensing when she places her hand on my chest. Luckily my kutte was zipped up, and I didn't rip my T-shirt because if it was unzipped, I might have had more than just a few scratches.

"This isn't funny, bikes are dangerous, and you could have been seriously hurt." The concern in her voice is assuring, with everything that has happened I wasn't sure if she actually liked me. Raising my hands to cup her cheeks, I lower my head to take her lips in a possessive but gentle kiss. I can't stay away from her any longer. I need her to know that I want her.

The kiss is all consuming, leaving both of us wanting more when I finally lift my head. Her eyes are half closed in passion. Her lips red and swollen from the kiss. Her breathing is choppy, as if she has just run a mile.

"Damn, you're a good kisser," she whispers and then immediately her cheeks flush, telling me that she didn't mean to blurt that out.

"You bring it out of me," I tease with a wink.

"I see you are a sweet talker, too." Before I can answer, there is a knock on the door. Sighing, I turn to open the door for Bion.

When he sees me, his eyes widen. "Looks like she can electrocute you after all," he teases.

"Very funny," I grunt, as I hear Siena laugh at his joke.

"Should I even ask?"

His question has me shaking my head as I unzip my Kutte and move to lay it down on the bed before looking down at my jeans. "I will clean those out before I start with your woman."

"They're fine."

"No, they not, you need to have them cleaned, you can get an infection," Siena's passionate cry has my eyes turning towards her displeased face. "Tell him, Bion." Being an Elemental, it's not very likely that I will get an infection from this, but I like having her worry about me, so I won't be the one to disappoint her.

"It won't hurt, I promise. I will even give you a lollipop after."

I raise my hand, showing Bion the finger.

"Come on, let's do this. Enough talk." I slide my arm under Siena's knees and the other behind her back. "Are you ready?" I ask, before lifting her.

"Not really, but it's fine."

Supporting her back as much as possible, I bring her leg up, pulling her close against my chest. Hearing her gasp in pain makes me hate myself for inflicting it on her, even if it was necessary.

"Lead the way. Where did you set up?" I ask.

"You will see." We head down the corridor and then turn towards the meeting room.

"No way, you set up in Church?" Tor isn't going to like that, he is very protective of certain things at the club, one of them is his hand-crafted oak meeting table with all the element symbols engraved on it.

"Yeah," Bion replies, glancing back at us with a grin. "Do you think Tor will mind?"

"You did this on purpose. He is going to have a fit." I shake my head in amusement. "You better hope he doesn't ban you from the club."

"Nah, he likes me too much," Bion teases as we walk in.

I see that he has placed a sheet over the table with a pillow on the far end.

"Place her stomach down, with her head to that side." He directs as he walks towards a haversack he has on a chair.

"Shouldn't there be a heart monitor, or blood, in case I need a transfusion or something?" I can hear the panic in Siena's voice as she sees the set up.

"Don't worry, baby girl, you are safer with Bion then any high-class surgeon." I can still see the doubt in her eyes when I sit her on the table. Lowering my head, I kiss her forehead, hating to see see her frightened expression.

"Are you going to stay here?" she whispers, making a knot tighten in my stomach. She trusts me—trusts me more than Bion, and she wants me here with her, which means that I give her comfort and confidence.

"Nothing could drag me away," I promise as I help her off with her T-shirt and then I help her lie down, turning her onto her stomach. Leaning over the table, I unhook her bra, hating the fact that another man will see her half naked.

I stand up straight, moving to the head of the table by her head. Placing my hand on her head, I stroke gently, trying to relax her nerves as much as possible. The scar and metal dial are stark against her pale skin, marring the silky smoothness.

Aldor is responsible for this. His evilness is the reason why she needs to go through all of this. I want to kill Aldor, but so does every other Elemental. I understand evil. I've even seen a lot of it throughout my very long life, but what he is responsible for is different. What is his purpose in doing this? In building an army of enhanced men? "Here, sweetheart, chew on this, please," Bion says as he pops what looks like a sugar sweet into her mouth.

"What is it?" she asks, sounding as if the sweet isn't very appetizing.

"Just a mixture of roots that will have you sleeping in no time," he promises as he looks down onto her back.

"It tastes like sand," she complains.

He smiles. "Yeah, so I've been told." I know that

whatever Bion will use is safe. I trust him completely and know that there is no one that knows roots better than him. I can hear Siena's heart slowing, telling me that the medicine Bion gave her is starting to take effect. A minute later, he is leaning forward until he is eye level with her.

"Can you hear me, Darling?" When there is no reply, he straightens. "Time to get this done."

"How long will she be out?" I ask, continuing stroking her head even though she can't feel it. I realize that it makes me feel better.

"Don't know. It's different with everyone." He places a brown well-worn leather pouch on the table, which he unwraps and extends to show a variety of medical tools. Fuck! Suddenly I wish I was anywhere but here. I have never been squeamish over blood, but the fact that he is going to cut into Siena has me grinding my teeth.

"Why don't you take a seat until I'm done?" Bion suggests as he bends over her back with a scalpel. He starts to slice the skin open a few inches above the metal piece. Immediately, blood pours out from where he cut. Then he cuts a few inches below. The smell of blood fills the air, and the sight of it has me squeezing my eyes shut to stop the urge I feel to jump Bion and stop him from doing that to her.

Even though I know that he's helping her, the fact that she is going to hurt because of it is messing with my head. The sloshy sound of his fingers opening up the flesh so that he can pull out the items has me grabbing onto the edge of the table with both hands.

I don't know how long I stand here like that, breathing in through my nose and out through my mouth, trying to calm myself so I don't jump him before he says. "Here it is. Those assholes are sick motherfuckers." Opening my eyes, I see him holding the round metal dial in his fingers. Five shortish thin metal tubes hang down with two sensors in the middle.

"Did you get it all out?" I ask.

"Yeah, but now I need to close her up before she wakes up." He stretches out his hand with the bloody piece of metal. "Here, hold this."

Taking it in my hand, I glare down at the offending piece of metal. Because of this gadget, Siena has been in pain for a while.

"Those two sensors you see in the middle capture information and send it out to whatever machine they have it synchronized with," Bion explains as he works on closing Siena up. Aldor must have spent a fortune to get everything set up. Whoever he has working on this is good and knows what they are doing. They are meticulous and have all their bases covered.

"Can you find the signal this is linked to?"

"Celmund is on it, because of everything that happened in Qatar the equipment they have might still be switched off. Trust me, as soon as that baby comes on, he will have a signal."

I place the piece on top of the table and look up to see Bion examining Siena's legs.

"What the fuck are you doing?"

"Making sure that she's fine. They did a lot of experiments on the women while they were there. I want to make sure there is nothing that will come to hurt her later." The anger that reared its head when seeing him touching my woman is reigning in.

"Is everything fine?" Bion doesn't answer immediately, but after he has finally examined everything, he looks up and nods.

"Now that I have taken that out of her back, she should be fine in no time, but I suggest that you share blood again as that will speed up her healing."

To know that my woman is going to be fine is a weight off my shoulders, a relief that is unexplainable. To love and to lose that person is a tragedy. But to love and not to live, that love is a crime. I will make sure that Siena will find that love with me, and that she will feel the joy of living a life filled with love.

SIENA 12

I can't believe it has been a week since Bion fixed my back. I only get a twinge now and again, but otherwise I'm moving around fine. Eirik has been amazing since the procedure. I never thought that I would get on as well as I do with him.

Anastasia, Esmeralda, and I are sitting outside under a tree as the weather is starting to warm, something which I missed while they had me locked away. It is amazing how we take things for granted when we have them every day. I glance towards the workshop to see Eirik bent over his Harley with a wrench in his hand as he takes off his pipes.

I look back at the women to see them both grinning at me.

"What?" I ask, as I feel my cheeks warming.

"You haven't heard a word I said, did you?" Anastasia asks.

"Of course, I did." Actually, I have no idea what they were talking about because ever since I came to sit outside my concentration has been on what is happening inside the workshop.

"That's good. Why don't you enlighten us because I wasn't saying anything, Esmeralda was," Anastasia says with a grin

I smile. "You can't blame me. I mean, look at him," I whisper as I incline my head towards the workshop.

"Yes, he does have a nice ass."

Anastasia's quip has me snapping around only to see that Eirik is behind his bike now. She was pulling my leg because he is nowhere where she can see his ass. Esmeralda and Anastasia burst out laughing at the speed at which I turned.

"Yeah, yeah, very funny," I mutter good naturedly.

"It's a good thing that he's a water bender. He can control all that drool when you look at him, so you won't drown." Esmeralda's comment has both guffawing again in merriment.

"Shhh, he will hear you," I whisper, glancing over my shoulder at the workshop, only to see Eirik grinning as he looks at us.

"Yeah, I think it's too late for that," Anastasia replies with a laugh. "But don't worry, he's coming this way to save you."

"What?" I swear I squeak out the word. I glance

back, only to see that Anastasia is telling the truth and Eirik is making his way towards us. His torso is glistening with sweat, and the tattoos that run the whole length of his body catch and hold your eye. The man is sculptured like a God, a mouth-watering morsel of a God.

"Are they giving you a hard time, baby girl?" he asks in an exaggerating stern voice which has the women laughing.

"What if we are? What will you do about it?" Anastasia asks.

"I guess I will have to complain to Dag and Ulrich so they can spank your naughty asses."

"Oh, please do," Anastasia replies in a pleading voice that has all of us laughing.

"You ladies are a bad influence on Siena. I think I need to take her away to keep her innocent purity intact." Eirik suddenly swoops down and lifts me up against his chest from where I was sitting. His musky odour fills my senses. My hand lifts to his chest, feeling the muscles rippling under my fingertips.

"Sure, if that's what you're calling it," Anastasia calls out as he turns his back on them and starts making his way inside.

"Are you really taking me inside?" I ask in surprise.

"Yeah, I can't wait any longer." His words have my mouth going dry when I think of what he could mean. Is he going to finally make love to me? After the procedure he has been having dinner with me and going to bed when I go, pulling me against his chest while I fall asleep.

We have kissed hot enough to scorch the sheets if he was a fire bender, but not hot enough to make him make love to me while I was healing. He insisted that he didn't want to hurt me, that he wanted our first time to be special, and that if I was in pain, it wouldn't be special at all.

I know that he wants me. Every time he has been near me, his erection is hard to miss. He even joked about it last night, saying that he would have to start wearing skirts soon to hide the tenting of his jeans. We have entered into an easy camaraderie, but I know that camaraderie will come to an end the minute I mention his past. I try to forget that he had a wife and try to think that it's me he wants—that he didn't love another woman.

To be fair, I don't know why I think like that because it's only right that he would have had other relationships because the man has lived for centuries, but what my head and my heart say is two completely different things. I know that it's unfair to expect him to have never wanted anyone in all those years, but my heart tells me, if I'm the one then how could he even consider being with another.

I had a relationship, one that I haven't mentioned because I realized that I never actually wanted him as a husband. But Eirik went as far as to marry the woman that he had a painting of above our bed.

"What's wrong, I can feel you tensing?" he asks, stopping just outside our bedroom.

"Nothing, I'm fine." I have been waiting for this moment for a long time now. I'm not going to say anything to ruin it.

"Are you sure?" he growls.

Lifting my hand, I place it on his cheek, feeling the heat from his skin running up my arm.

"I'm sure."

His eyes are so intense, and I can see the uncertainty on his face as he looks down at me. Sliding my fingers up his neck, I pull his head down until his lips are touching mine. "I'm sure," I murmur again.

The passion he unleashes leaves me gasping for breath. He walks us into the room, and I only realize it when he is laying me down on the bed. His hands slide up my torso, pulling my T-shirt off in the process. "I've been imagining this since the day I met you."

My hands lower to the band of my tights, pulling them down as he unzips his jeans. His eyes watch every move I make, running over my body like a scorching beam, branding every inch as his. When he takes a step towards the bed, I'm sitting there in my panties and nothing else. My eyes run over his beautiful body, the tattoos are hypnotizing as I look down over his chest and torso until I get to his waist. My eyes widen when I see that he has a piercing on his penis.

Oh my word, the man looks like he was made for sex.

"Umm, won't that hurt if… umm… you know?"

He looks down at himself. His hand slides around his well-endowed piece, sliding it up and down a few times. The movement is more erotic than anything I have ever seen.

I can feel the moisture pooling between my legs as I watch him. "You mean if you do this?" he asks in a deep, passion-filled voice. The drop of wetness at the tip is like a hypnotic crystal holding my gaze. My tongue flickers out to moisten my lips.

"You want me, don't you?" he asks, taking a step closer.

I nod, not being able to speak through the knot in my throat. I want this man more than I thought it was possible to ever want anyone like this. I have only had sex with two other men before, and both those men didn't make me weak at the knees like Eirik does with a simple look.

He places his knee on the bed, leaning slightly forward as he picks up my hand, placing it where his hand was a moment ago, making me stroke his impressive girth. I am fascinated with the twinkling of the piercing every time my hand strokes back. His muscles are straining as he lets me get acquainted with his body. Lifting my eyes, I meet his intense gaze, his eyes slightly close with passion, his lips parted as he enjoys every stroke.

"Lay back." His voice is low and laced with passion. With a promise of things to come.

I reluctantly let go of him and stretch out.

His eyes travel over my body, slowly making sure to familiarize himself with every beauty spot, every dent, and cranny. "You are beautiful." His words boost my confidence, and the evidence of his erect penis confirms he's telling the truth.

He leans down to stroke the tips of his fingers around my stomach and up to my nipples that are erect with desire. My skin is sensitive to his touch, and then he suddenly flicks his tongue over the sensitive nub which has me gasping at the flash of desire that shoots through my body.

"Kiss me," I murmur, needing his lips on me.

He smiles knowingly as he bends over me, his lips hovering an inch above mine. "You're a passionate little thing, aren't you?"

I'm about to answer him when his lips touch down on mine. First lightly and then more intensely. A feeling of rightness surrounds me in its embrace. This whole mating business could be what is igniting the fervour I feel for this man, but only a dead woman wouldn't find him desirable, or want to be possessed by someone like him. With his intense magnetism that draws you in.

His hands roam my body. Feeling its firmness, his fingers slide over my skin like a feather, igniting my senses. His kiss is all-consuming as our tongues dance to a rhythm older than time. I feel like my body is more alive at this moment than it has ever been in my whole life.

"Eirik," I whisper as he moves to kiss my neck. His warm breath has goosebumps raising across my skin. His teeth nip at my shoulder just as I feel a tug on my panties. The ripping sound so loud in the silence of the room. He raises up on his knees, pulling at what's left of the blue panties I was wearing and dropping them on the bed next to me.

"Mine!" The growled word is said in a deep no nonsense tone that leaves no doubt in my mind that he completely accepts it. His hand runs up my calf to my thigh, and then he is touching me deeply with the pads of his fingers, rubbing gently at my very core, igniting a turbulent wave of desire that has me wanting more.

He slides one of his fingers deep within my body, feeling my readiness, feeling the beckoning of my body for his. His eyes never leave my face, drinking every expression, every murmur of pleasure that he is wringing out of me.

I don't know how long he tortures me with the expectation of our union before he is slotting himself between my knees, his face a mirror of raw passion, intense and all consuming. When I feel the tip of his cock sliding over my folds, the coldness of his piercing is a contrast to the scolding heat that our two bodies are radiating.

I close my eyes, my torso rising as he slides slowly and so deeply inside me. My hands grab the duvet, clasping at it as a false sense of safety. The things his body is making me feel have me scared that I will shatter into a million pieces and never be able to be put back together again if I don't hold on with all my might.

"Look... at... me!" he orders with each thrust of his body.

Opening my eyes, I am caught in his gaze, his intense desire there for me to see. "Now and forever, Siena."

His words are a promise that he seals as he joins his lips with mine. His body still thrusting and retreating with hard deep thrusts, building up the tremors that have started deep within my very core.

"Eirik!" I gasp as I feel the deluge of emotions, of unbridled lust, overwhelm every fibre of my being. "Eir... ik! I scream as the control I was trying to hold on to vanishes, and in its place is a wild, uncontrolled avalanche of feelings.

"Yes," he whispers. "Yes!" Louder. "Oh fuck!" he roars. Everything around me seems suspended in time, as I'm completely consumed by this moment in time. I know deep in my soul that there might be problems in the future, but for now it's just me and Eirik, and its perfect.

***

I must have passed out, or fallen asleep, because the next thing I know I am being awakened by a flaming hot sensation across my back. Oh no, did I hurt my back? I can hear a thundering in my ear, a thundering that I realize is Eirik's heart as my head is laying on his chest. How I got there I have no recollection as the last thing I remember is him lowering to kiss me sweetly.

Sitting up, I try to reach the top of my back to gather if I somehow injured or opened the area that Bion fixed.

"Siena?" Eirik asks in a sleepy tone. But when I look at him, I see his eyes are alert.

"My back is burning. Please, see if I hurt it?" No sooner are the words out of my mouth, he is behind me looking at my back, his hand running over my skin. "Argh" I gasp, the skin sensitive to the touch.

"Don't move, let me see," he orders. A minute later he is sighing with what sounds like relief.

"Eirik?"

"It's okay baby girl, you didn't hurt yourself." He kisses my shoulder tenderly, as I feel cool air on my back as he blows gently.

"What are you doing?" I ask, stiffening but don't move as the cool air actually seems to be helping.

"You are getting my mark, baby girl. The heat will go away soon, just relax." What? what does he mean his mark? Freya and Anastasia showed me the marks they have. They said it's their mating mark. The tattoo like marks they have, each on a different part of their bodies, but I thought they got tattoos done, not that it burns its way onto your body when you sleep with your mate.

Anastasia and Freya's tattoos, or what Eirik calls marks, are beautiful, intricate patterns that they explained look exactly like the ones Ulrich and Dane were born with. Eirik's body is covered in tattoos. I wouldn't know which are his marks, I just hope it's not a skull or something similar.

"Show me."

Eirik raises a brow in question, but then he is turning slightly and pointing towards his arm.

"The Crow?" I gasp in shock, it's a beautiful imitation of a crow's head. It's eyes intense as they look out at everyone, but I don't want a damn crow on my body.

"What? No," he replies as he runs his finger along his shoulder down to his elbow. I realize what he's showing me is the intricate swirls that seem to look like infinity strokes woven into a space of lines, a pattern that pulls you in with its beauty.

"That will be my pattern?" I ask in surprise, pleased that it's not one of his other more graphic ones.

"Yes, that's my birth mark."

"How long will it take for the whole thing to appear?" The heat on my back is already starting to ease, but there is still a slight tenderness. That type of mark will probably take a while even for this crazy type of magic they have.

Eirik stops blowing to look at my back before answering. "It's all there, I would say a couple more minutes."

"What," I gasp in surprise, "already?" Eirik doesn't reply. Instead, he slides his hand around my neck pulling me to him and locking our lips together, in a possessive all-consuming kiss.

EIRIK 13

"You know, that this is fucking freaky," Tal suddenly says from next to me. He offered to help me with the new tank for my bike. I decided that after the accident I might as well get the artwork I wanted done on my tank as it was going to be out of commission for a while, as I fixed all the odds and ends to it. Bjarni, who is a brother in our mother chapter, is an absolute genius when it comes to the artwork on our rides, just sent me the tank with what I asked, and I couldn't wait to get it fitted.

"What's wrong, don't you like it?" I think he did a great job with the E and S intertwined in flames.

"It's not that. Will you fucking stop smiling? It's starting to scare me."

His teasing has me grinning as I show him the finger.

It's true, I have found myself smiling more. I feel more at peace with an appetite for life that I haven't had for a very long time.

I didn't want a mate, but now I can't think of my life without Siena. Her exuberant personality brings a static energy to the club that seems to liven everything up. "I'm glad you found her, Bro." Tal's sudden serious tone has me glancing at him. "We were worried about you. It was evident that you were giving up. So, if finding your mate has brought you back to us, I'm all for Siena smoking your ass every now and again to see if you're still kicking."

I know that the others were worried about me, and that they were concerned that I would let my darkness take me. But I was prepared to end my life before I let that happen. I have seen too many Elementals that turned Keres to let that shit happen to me. Men that I knew for a very long time, giving up and letting their basic instincts overcome them. Finding Siena was a blessing, one that I am aware I am lucky to have had.

I know that she's still wary about my marriage. We don't talk about it, but it's there in the background. Two days ago, I finally made her fully mine. Every inch of her belongs to me, like I belong to her. The connection between us is better than I could ever have wished for. I know that the bond between mates is unbreakable, that the union is like nothing else, but I never knew that it would consume me completely.

"I think your woman's parents are here."

Tal's statement has me turning towards the sound of the car driving up towards the club. Siena phoned her parents last night, wanting to make sure that she was fine before contacting them. She didn't want them to worry when they saw her. "You better go meet your in-laws."

"Yeah." This is something that I could happily do without, I am not a people person, and having to sit through a civil conversation with people that I clearly have nothing in common with is not something which I am looking forward to, but I know that it will make Siena happy, so I will nod at the right times and hopefully they will leave soon.

Picking up the rag from the seat of my bike, I clean my hands before sighing.

"Just smile, dude. Trust me, and they will leave real quick worried that you might eat them." Tal's absurd statement has me looking at him in surprise. His innocent expression makes me grin.

"You're a mad motherfucker, do you know that?"

My comment has him shrugging as he inclines his head towards the door. Shaking my head, I head out of the workshop and towards the red Ford which a middle-aged couple are now getting out of.

I see the couple looking around with a worried look

on their faces. "Oh my, why is she here?" the mother says in a worried voice.

"You're here!"

I stop as Siena comes out of the club, hurrying towards the couple.

"Slow down, damn," I grunt, as I make it to her before she can hurt herself. Even though she's moving fine, there is still a possibility of her hurting herself.

"Oh!" Siena gasps as I slide my arms around her waist just as she's about to trip over the last step. "Eirik," she whispers in surprise.

"Be careful," I grunt, pulling her tight against me.

"Siena," the woman calls as she reaches us, her eyes wide as she looks at us

"Mama," Siena replies as she pulls away from me and throws herself into her mothers' arms.

"Oh, Siena, I was so worried," she whispers, hugging her close.

"Siena."

I tense as the man walks behind her. "Where have you been, Chicka? You had us worried."

"Papa," she cries as she turns into the man's embrace. Her happiness is a pleasure to see, and If I have to sit through a whole week behaving for her sake, then so be it. I see the mother looking at me curiously, but I don't introduce myself. Instead, I wait patiently for Siena to greet her parents. I know the other women are standing behind me because I can sense their energy. They have all grown a tight bond amongst themselves. It's clear to see that they are happy for Siena's happiness.

A few minutes later, Siena is finally stepping back and turning towards me, her face radiant with happiness. "I want you to meet Eirik. He's the one that saved me when I was kidnapped." Siena mentioned the kidnapping to her parents when she phoned, but she didn't tell them everything that happened to her.

Her dad approaches with his hand out. "Thank you so much, young man. I don't know what we would have done if anything happened to Siena."

I take his hand nodding; I didn't expect thanks, but for some reason the fact that my woman's dad likes me is somewhat comforting.

"Why don't you go inside? I'm sure you will be more comfortable there," I say, wanting to get them out of the way when I hear motorcycle engines making their way towards us.

"Oh, of course," Siena says as she comes to stand in the middle of her parents, sliding her arm through theirs as she starts to steer them inside introducing them to the other women that are standing by the door. Catching Anastasia's eye, I incline my head inside just as I hear the roar of the bikes come to a stop near the gate.

"How about something to drink, come on inside," Anastasia calls, catching my meaning.

"We aren't expecting anyone, are we?" Tal asks with a raised brow as he stops next to me.

"Not that I'm aware of," I reply just as Tor and Garth walk towards us from inside.

"We've got company. Looks like the Savage Cobras MC are at our gates," Tor calls as he comes to join us. "Stay sharp, we can't trust those motherfuckers."

"Do you know what they want?" Garth asks, looking like that he still hasn't slept since arriving from Qatar yesterday. His hair is dishevelled, and he's still wearing the same clothes he arrived in. Haldor wasn't happy about having to come back home yet, but it seemed like all the leads had dried up there.

"No, but we are about to find out," Tor replies just

as five of the Savage Cobras come riding up towards us. Their bikes come to a stop a few feet before us. We have had dealings with the Savage Cobras before, but it has never been a club that we entertain much because they dabble in a lot of things that we aren't interested in. Their leader is a twitchy son of a bitch that sniffs way too much of his own product if you ask me.

"Jed, what brings you to my door?" Tor asks their leader as Jed takes off his helmet. His thinning, oily, dark hair is plastered to his head.

"I was hoping for one of your parties, no one throws a party like you guys," he says with a wink, but it's clear that he's here for another reason, a reason I'm sure we will find out about in due time.

"Afraid we not throwing a party. If you haven't heard we are at war with the gangs and can't be too careful." Jed and the others that have now parked their bikes start making their way towards us.

"I've heard the rumours," Jed remarks with a shrug. "A shame, but I would like to talk to you about something that might just interest you."

Tor raises a brow. I doubt that anything Jed wants to propose we'll be interested in.

"But first, it has been a really thirsty ride," he says

with a grin.

Tor scowls, but he reluctantly nods before turning. "Okay, Jed, but I have shit to do, so this better not take too long," Tor warns as he starts making his way inside.

I would have rather avoided going in at al because Siena and her parents are sitting in the bar area as we walk in.

I see their eyes widen at the company. Siena's mom leans towards her, whispering, "Are you sure you want to stay here? I don't think this is the most appropriate place for you."

Tal elbows me, a grin lighting his face. "Doesn't look like the mom thinks we are good enough for her daughter," he murmurs so softly as to not to be overheard by the Savage Cobras.

"Shhh, they will hear you," Siena replies with a gasp. "And trust me, this is the safest place for me."

I glance at her to see her eyes trained on me. I know that she would have liked her parents to get to know me, but with the Savage Cobras here, it's important that I stay close because I don't trust these assholes.

"Well now, you have been holding out on the rest of us, Bro," Rev, one of the Savage Cobra's men, calls out to Garth.

"How's that?" Garth asks.

"Those beauties weren't here the last time I came here. They sure are pretty." My eyes turn to him, the anger starting to rise when I realize that he's talking about our Ol' Ladies. If he's not careful, he will be leaving here seeing less than when he came in.

"Those aren't for your palate, they are Ol' Ladies," Tal replies as the men start taking their seats.

"Aww, come on, I share my Ol' Lady." His meaning has me leaning forward as I grab his shirt and pull him close to me until his face is a foot away from mine.

"We don't!" I warn.

His eyes widen as he raises both his hands. "Okay, dude, no need to get touchy," he mutters as I let go.

"Rev, take a seat and shut the fuck up," Jed calls.

"Camille," Tor calls out for one of our Jezebels that is working behind the bar today. He circles his finger around the table, letting her know that he wants a round of drinks. She nods, leaning down to pull out the bottles of beer and placing them on the tray.

"Well, Jed, what do you want to talk about?" Tor

asks.

Jed looks around and then shrugs. "I think it's better if we talk in private."

"I don't keep secrets from my men, so you might as well get to it." Jed doesn't seem happy with Tor's decision, but he knows better than to contradict him.

"We have a business proposition," he says in a soft voice. I notice his guys must know about the business offer because they aren't paying him any attention and rather their eyes keep on roaming about, especially in the women's direction which is starting to piss me off.

"We have someone that wants guns."

I see Tor tense; our main influx of money comes from the weapons that we transport for the Bratva Fury mafia family. It isn't something we announce to anyone, and we are weary when someone comes calling talking about weapons.

"Why would you think I have guns?" Tor asks.

"No," Jed replies as he leans closer to Tor. "We don't want guns from you, we just want backup."

"You're shitting me?" Tor asks in an amused voice.

"No, man. Seriously, these guys, they don't play

around," Jed confides, sounding a little weary.

"If you don't trust them, then why are you getting into bed with them?" Tor asks with a raised brow as he folds his arms across his chest.

"They didn't really give me a choice," he confesses. "Come on, man. I know they wouldn't try anything if you were there."

"Going for a leak," Terrence, one of Jed's men says as he stands, making his way towards the back where we have the bathroom. I keep my eyes on him as he goes towards the corridor. I don't trust these assholes.

"Who are they?" Garth asks from where he's sitting next to Rev.

"I can't tell you that unless you agree to help us." Jed responds.

"Well, then we can't help you as I can't make a decision unless I know all the details," Tor's reply has Jed tensing.

"Wha…" The distressed sound has me snapping out of my chair. Garth, Tal and Tor have also stood. Garth and Tal are standing over Jed's men threateningly as I make my way towards where I heard the sound. Tor is right behind me as we round the corner to find Terrence with his hand over

Esmeralda's mouth, a knife lifting to her neck.

Before he can stab her, I have moved in the blink of an eye and grabbed his wrist. "Motherfucker, you have no idea what you were about to do," I growl, wanting to string him up by his balls, but leaving that to Dag that is going to skin this son of a bitch for thinking he could touch his mate.

"Sweetheart, are you okay?" Tor asks as I pull Terrence against the wall away from Esmeralda. I can see her frightened expression as she stares at Terrence. "Esmeralda?" Tor calls when she doesn't answer.

"Ye..." she starts to say, but then gulps before continuing. "Yes, I'm okay."

"Hold them!" Tor suddenly roars, the anger vibrating through him. He pulls out his phone from his back pocket, looking down at it as he grunts before answering. "She's fine," he says before Dag has a chance to answer, "but I want you back pronto, there is a situation you are going to want to sort out." Being mated, we know when our women are distressed. Dag must have felt Esmeralda's fear and contacted Tor. I can just imagine his anxiety thinking that something was happening to his woman.

"Yes, I'm sure she's fine. Now stop wasting time

and get here." Tor says again before disconnecting the call. "Freya!" he calls.

A minute later Freya is hurrying towards us, her expression cautious as she looks at the fucker I am holding. "Sweetheart, why don't you take Esmeralda outside for some air, also make sure Eirik's in laws go with you.

Shit, I forgot about them. This was the worst timing ever to try to appease them that Siena will be safe with me. Pulling Terrance forward, I once again push him hard against the wall. "Why?" I ask quietly next to his ear, not wanting the others to hear.

"Tor, come on; we can talk this out."

Tor turns towards Jed that is being held back by Tal. "You came here for this?" Tor asks quietly— too quietly. Anyone that knows Tor knows that this is the calm before the storm, and if you are clever, you will get the fuck out of Dodge before that storm explodes.

"We didn't have an option; you need to believe me," Jed pleads in a whining voice. "They would have ended us."

Tor starts walking towards him, his body vibrating in anger. I pull Terrance forward, sliding my arm around his neck to subdue his struggles as I push him forward, noticing that the women and Siena's parents have left.

Good, I don't want my woman to witness anymore violence. She has had enough in her short life. Tor comes to a stop before Jed that gulps in nervousness. "You come into my club and try to kill one of our Ol' Ladies. What did you think was going to happen to you?" Tor's words start out softly but by the end they are filled with fury as his hands snap out and he lifts Jed off his feet by his Kutte.

"Don't fucking move, asshole, or I'll lay you out right now," Garth orders as he pulls one of the other guys back into his chair that was about to stand.

Jed tries to kick Tor to break free, but Tor throws him back, which has him landing with a loud thwack on a table that cracks and breaks under his weight. Terrance decides to try his luck by elbowing me on my side, which just serves to ignite my anger even more. If he wasn't Dag's, he would be dead already.

Tightening my hold around his neck, I whisper, "You will be dead soon enough, asshole, so enjoy your last moments." Just then I hear the roar of bikes outside, which announces the arrival of Dag and the others. "Looks like your time is up."

Jed is starting to sit up just as Haldor, Einar and Colborn walk inside. "Shit, man, I liked that table," Colborn says conversationally as he goes to stand behind Jed. Seeing as Dag isn't with them it means that he must have seen Esmeralda and gone to make sure she is fine before coming inside.

"What happened?" Einar asks.

"These assholes came here professing to have a business proposition for us, but as soon as Esmeralda walked inside, that son of a bitch over there decided he wanted to cut her," Tal explains as he inclines his head towards Terrance and me.

"Who sent them?" Colborn asks as he places his hands on his waist, looking down at Jed.

"Haven't got to that yet," Tor replies.

"Oh, I see, just having some fun first," Colborn states with a wink just as Dag appears in the doorway, his body tense with fury, his expression murderous as he takes in the group before him.

"Who?"

Esmeralda must have told him what happened, because he doesn't ask. Tor points towards me, and Dag's eyes snap to us. I let go of Terrence, knowing that his time is limited. You do not touch one of our mates and leave breathing, especially a mate carrying our child.

"Now look, boys, this is what happens when you touch one of our Ol' Ladies," Tal calls out to the three men still sitting at the table with Garth standing over them. Dag is making his way towards Terrence, each step a death toll.

"Fuck off," Terrance roars as he charges Dag, throwing a punch as he gets close, a punch that Dag stops with his hand, holding his fist tightly.

"You want to hurt my woman, frighten her?" His voice is laced with rage. "You will die for touching her." Then I hear bones cracking, and Terrance is shouting in pain as Dag breaks the bones in his hand. Dag's free hand snaps out, grabbing Terrance around the neck, lifting him off the floor as he lets go of his now broken hand.

The other Savage Cobra men try to intervene but are quickly immobilized. Terrance is gasping for breath as Dag holds him up by his neck, squeezing slowly until his lips turn blue and his eyes are rolling back. Finally, he twitches and gasps out his last breath. Letting go of Terrance's neck, Dag lets him fall to the ground, dead.

"Now, who sent you?" Tor asks as he goes to stand before Jed that is cowering on the ground.

"Basil... Basil sent us," Jed screams. "We owe them. If we didn't do this, they would have ended us." Tor looks at Colborn nodding for him to pick Jed up. Looks like those assholes haven't given up, even after all this time. We thought that by killing Sean, the previous Desperados' leader, that they would leave Esmeralda alone, but it looks like revenge is ingrained in their DNA because they insist on trying to kill her.

After escaping and stealing the Desperados' ledger, Esmeralda buried them by giving it to us. We were able to put an end to their trafficking of women with Aldor, something which they aren't happy about as that seemed to be one of their main venues of income. We also destroyed most of their drug houses which at the time was a big blow for them because they lost product, men, and their clients went somewhere else.

"I'm going to kill that son of a bitch," Dag states, looking at Tor.

"Yes, it's time we stop the Desperados completely," Tor snaps as he pulls Jed towards him. "And now it's time for us to tango. Take these wankers outside, I don't want blood in the club." He shakes Jed a few times before pushing him into Colborn's arms. "Eirik, you and Haldor sort this mess out, and get rid of that piece of shit," he orders, inclining his head towards Terrance.

Shit, I hate getting rid of fucking bodies, why don't humans just disintegrate into the elements like we do when we die?

SIENA 14

It was nice to have my parents here; to see them again, even though I had to try to appease them over what they saw today. It doesn't usually happen or, at least, I hope it doesn't. It took a lot of convincing from my side for my parents to finally agree to leave without me. Maybe next time I see them it would be better if it were away from the club.

I felt terrible for Esmeralda, but even though she was a little shaken, she seemed to take it quite well. But after the little bit that I've heard about her past, it's understandable that she is used to violence. Dag was furious. It was clear to see after she explained what happened and his expression filled with murderous rage. He asked Freya to take her to her room to rest, which she refused the minute he left, saying that she was fine and that the fresh air was all she needed.

"Does this happen often?" I ask Anastasia as we make our way back towards the club, entering through the back as not to disturb the men.

"We are at war, but no, it doesn't really come this close to us," she says as she slides her arm through mine. "I like your parents."

"Thanks, they just worry about me."

"It's understandable."

"Would anyone else like to go for a swim? I think that's what I need," Esmeralda suddenly says as she stops near the door to the inside pool.

"You know," Freya replies, "I think that's actually a good idea. I could use a nice glass of wine while I relax."

"Now you're talking, I'll go get the wine and a juice for you." Anastasia says, smiling at Esmeralda as she pulls away from me. "You guys go on in."

"I don't have anything to swim with." My clothes haven't been collected from my apartment yet, which has left me with borrowed clothes that the others have kindly let me use.

"I'll tell you what. Let's all be naughty and go swimming with our underwear, as I don't feel like having to go and change now."

I know that Freya is just being nice because of my lack of clothes, but I nod with a smile as I open the door to where the interior pool and gym are. It still amazes me at the lavishness that Tor has put into everything at the club. Sometimes I still doubt that

I'm in a motorcycle club when I see some of the things that they have, like this interior pool with its beautiful interior plants, the sauna, and the gym with everything we could ever want.

Eirik said that Tor was some kind of Viking lord in his day, and it's easy to see by the way lives. I still haven't been here for one of their parties, but Anastasia and Freya say that it's an experience that one never forgets because they doubt anyone else has parties like Tor does.

Apparently, since the war started with the Desperados, there have been no more parties because they worry about the security, and today goes to prove that anyone can be a foe. Pulling off my T-shirt, I lay it down on one of the loungers next to the pool. My tan-coloured bra is not exactly sexy lingerie, but it will do. The problem is that I have a G-string on which don't cover as much as I would like them to, but the women have seen me naked before when they used to help me into the shower and out, therefore I'm not as self-conscious as I would have been a few months ago.

"I hope I look like you when I get pregnant." Freya says

Turning to look at Esmeralda that has just sat on one of the loungers in a black bra and panties, I smile. It's true, Esmeralda has a small baby bump, but she looks so cute pregnant, that anyone would wish to have a child to look like that.

"When are you planning on that happening?" Esmeralda asks as she lays back, sighing.

"I don't know. You know what they say about the Elementals. When it has to happen, it will." Yes, they have mentioned that contraception doesn't work where elementals are concerned and that pregnancies only happen when the time is right. There are some couples that go years without a child sometimes and then one day they are pregnant. There are others like Dag and Esmeralda that fall pregnant immediately.

Bion assured me that a pregnancy won't be a problem, and that all the experiments they did didn't ruin my possibility of pregnancy. When I think about Eirik and what a great father he will be, it makes me smile. I still have my doubts sometimes about the fact that he only wants me because I'm his mate, even though the woman he actually loved was his wife.

Just the thought of him loving someone else fills me with sadness, he shows me all the care and passion any woman would be more than happy with, but is it real? Does he love me as much as he loved his wife? "I got us one white and one red," Anastasia says as she walks towards us, a bottle in each hand,

and I see a juice bottle under her arm, drawing me away from my depressing thoughts.

"I prefer the white." I call out.

"I don't mind either," Freya replies with a shrug.

"Looks like I don't have a choice," Esmeralda quips as she sees the juice.

"Nope," Anastasia replies, handing her the juice.

"What about glasses?" Freya asks.

"I didn't have any more hands; we can swig it from the bottle."

At her serious expression, I burst out laughing. "Very sexy," I reply. "Give it here then. Let me be the first on this downfall of womanhood," I joke as I lift the bottle and take a gulp of the wine. "Mmm, this is actually really good wine."

"What do you expect, only the best for Tor," Freya states as she takes the bottle from me. "Not that I'm complaining."

"When he finds his woman, he will lavish her with presents," Anastasia says, smiling.

"That's true. I have noticed that about him. He likes to give people gifts," Esmeralda says, her eyes still closed as she relaxes with her head back against her lounger. "Every month since I found out that I was pregnant, he has given us something for the baby."

"Oh, what did you get?" I ask curiously.

"I have received a baby set of gold cutlery. They were really beautiful, with all the elements engraved on it. A gold bracelet that made me laugh because it looks so much like one of the ones he wears and that there is no way the poor kid would be able to wear it with the weight of the gold. Then this month I received a small crate that you will see in the workshop. It's a miniature Harley that apparently kids can ride when they are four and older."

"A Harley?" Freya asks in surprise. "No way?"

"Oh yes," Esmeralda confirms.

"Dag thought it was great and was upset because he didn't think of it first. I didn't tell him that there is no way that our kid is going to ride a motorcycle at that age." I know that if the Elementals have girls, the girls don't get their father's powers of bending the elements, but the boys always get an element.

"If it's a girl, do they get a gift like we do?" I know what my gift has cost me, and I don't think I would like my daughter to go through the same problems that I went through.

"Yes, I think so," Freya replies as she stands to step

into the pool. "This water is always so nice and warm."

Esmeralda opens her eyes, a smile lifting her lips.

"I think I'll join you," she says as she stands.

"Yeah, why not," I murmur, also standing. I haven't been to a swimming pool since I was a kid. Walking to the edge, I jump in, splashing Anastasia that squeals as she jumps back.

"Oh, you going to pay for that," she laughs as she turns towards my lounger and grabs my clothes.

"No!" I scream with a laugh. "I will be walking out of here with a naked ass."

"Oh, well, I guess you better run," Anastasia says with a laugh as she drops it into the pool.

"Oh man." I laugh as I lunge for my clothes, but they are already sinking into the pool. Diving under I bring them up, throwing them at Anastasia, they hit her with a sloshing sound.

"Well, looks like I am going to be coming in after all," she says as she pulls off her jeans to display a lacy pair of panties that don't leave much to anyone's imagination.

"Nice panties," Freya teases.

"Yeah, well I'm coming in with my T-shirt as I don't have a bra on," she replies as she comes to stand at the edge of the pool and then dives in just like a professional swimmer.

"Show off," I call as I swim towards Esmeralda and pull myself up to sit next to her. "I bomb in, she dives in like a mermaid."

Esmeralda laughs at my teasing.

I haven't had a day like this in an exceedingly long while. Ever since I left school and started working, I lost touch with most of my school friends, but even if I still saw them, they were never those friends that you hear about that people go through their whole life with the same best friend. I always believed that a real friend is one that you can trust completely—the one that you know that no matter what, they'll stand by you, and are there for better or worse.

These three women seem to be the real deal and if I am going to hang around here, I think if we are going to be good friends. I can't think of myself being away from Eirik. What they say is true because I think about him all the time. When he touches me, it's like I come alive, like everything around me doesn't matter. When I look at Esmeralda, it has my heart jump with excitement that one day my dream will become a reality and I will finally have a family.

Placing my hand on Esmeralda's shoulder, I stroke it gently. "How are you feeling after what happened?" I would still be shaking if it were me. But it seems like Esmeralda is taking it in stride.

"I'm okay. I was just worried about the little one. But it's been kicking up a fuss, so I'm all good." Her smile is sad as she looks at me. "Dag was furious."

"Yes, he was, but he had every right. Look at what could have happened."

She nods at my words and then smiles as Freya swims up to us, splashing us lightly before swimming away again.

"I heard him talking to Tor. He said that he promised me that I would never be around violence again and that he has failed." She sounds so sad. "I don't want him to feel like that." Sliding my arm around her shoulders, I hug her close.

I think because of what happened to me and Esmeralda's past, we have gotten close. There is an aura around Esmeralda of old wisdom.

Just then, Haldor walks through the door with a scowl on his face. I met him for the first time when they arrived yesterday. It's clear that he's hurting, and the death of his sister is devastating to him, but he's closing himself off with anger.

"Hey, Haldor?" he stops on his way to the gym to look back at Anastasia. "Is everything over with now?"

He frowns, but nods.

"Why don't you come for a swim with us, Haldor? I haven't seen you in such a long time."

His frown turns into a scowl. "I need to train," he mutters as he turns, making his way into the gym and closing the door behind himself.

Anastasia looks at us, shaking her head sadly. It's sad when you see someone hurting, but you can't do anything to help that person. Standing, I make my way towards my lounger only to stop when the door to the pool area opens again, and Eirik, Dag, and Ulrich walk in.

"So, this is where you have all go…" Eirik starts and then he is rushing towards me. "What the fuck?"

His surprised statement has me jumping in surprise as his arms slide around me from behind and he is pulling me flush against his body. A growl emits from his throat as he turns us, so his back is to the pool, and I am standing facing the plants on the far wall. "You are practically naked!" His voice is angry, leading me to believe that he didn't like the fact that I'm wandering about in my G-string.

"Hey, babe," Anastasia calls just as I hear Ulrich swearing.

"Shit, your fucking T-shirt is see-through."

"Stand still," Eirik grunts as I try to break free. Then he is loosening his grip as he pulls his T-shirt off. Turning to face him, I yelp as he starts to pull it over my head.

"What the hell are you doing?" I ask angrily, as I try to smack his hands away.

"There are other men here, you know? They don't need to fucking see you naked." His voice is growling with anger, his muscles ripping as he pulls the shirt over my body until it is midway down my thighs. I can hear the other women also arguing with their men, as they all seem to have a problem with what we are wearing, except for Dag. I can see from the corner of my eye that he's hugging Esmeralda close as he nuzzles her neck.

"You're such a savage," I mutter. "You do know that we are in the twentieth century, and I am sure that the men in this club have seen more than their fair share of naked women, including you."

"But none of those women were mine," he growls angrily, which has me placing my hands on my waist as I glare up at him.

"Really, what about your dear wife?" I say in anger before stepping around him and hurrying towards the door, which I don't make because he is suddenly standing before me.

"Where the fuck did that come from?" he growls as a muscle twitches near his eyebrow.

"Just forget it," I reply as I try to step around him, but he grabs my arm, his eyes hard as he looks down at me.

"No, I don't think so."

And then the next minute I am being picked up and we are making our way out of the pool area as soon as the door closes the other couple's angry voices are silenced and all I can hear is my thundering heart beating in my ears.

"Put me down, I can walk," I order.

He ignores me as he continues making his way into our room before slamming the door shut with the heel of his boot and dropping me onto the mattress. He stands over me like an avenging angel, his hands low on his waist, his biceps flickering with tension, and his expression intense.

This conversation has been brewing ever since the day I found out that he was married before, and now it has come to a head. Will he be able to appease this feeling of betrayal I feel? I know it's silly, feeling like this when it was before my time, but it's stronger than me.

EIRIK 15

"I can't change the past," I roar in frustration. Fuck, right now I would gladly do anything to make her happy. Did I make a mistake in thinking that Isabela could ever be my mate? Yes, because the feelings that are engraved in my soul for Siena are nothing like what I felt for Isabela.

I berate myself over the hope I gave Isabela—for the dream of a fairy-tale that in reality could never be and was false. I know that now. I tried to do the best I could. I tried to fight for that love, that nirvana that some of the other Elementals found—thinking that I had found it, not knowing any better. But deep down, I was still empty inside—still dark. I felt more at peace with the fact that I was loved, and that maybe somehow, I had found that eternal balm of happiness.

"Do you even want to?" Siena asks angrily as she sits up, glaring at me. "Someone that is supposed to be searching for his one true mate sure doesn't care about that when he has a picture of another woman hanging in his room for years, Eirik. Years!"

I throw up my hands in anger as I snap around. "Fuck, Siena," I roar in anger, taking in a deep breath as I try to calm myself before I turn around again.

"Isabela was good to me. She wasn't my mate, but she treated me right." I take in a deep breath. "She was my past and I feel bad that I could never give her the depth of commitment that I feel for you." Taking a step closer, I point at her. "You, Siena, it's fucking you I want. Not a past that wasn't real."

"But you had her painting and looked at it every day."

"Yes, I hung it up, but after a while I didn't even notice it."

I won't lie to Siena; she has a right to know the truth and hopefully after everything, we will forget about my marriage and carry on with our lives. "When I met Isabela, I was in a dark place. My parents had just died, and I couldn't see any goodness around me. That is, until I met her. Isabela was a carefree creature that did everything to make everyone around her happy. I had never met someone that was so pure at heart, so willing to do anything for others."

"Isn't that nice," Siena says sarcastically as she stands.

"No, it's not nice," I snap as I grab her arm. "What I'm trying to say is that I loved her for the carefree love she gave me. For saving me from darkness. At that point in time, I thought, what the hell? She made me feel normal, so why not give her a better life? All she wanted was to have a family, and I was lost at the time. I wanted to love her—wanted to give her what she wanted and hated the fact that I was an Elemental and no matter how much I tried I just couldn't." Siena tries to pull away from me, but I tighten my hold. "I never felt for her like I feel for you. I never wanted her as much as I want you and I have never been as fucking obsessed with anyone like I am with you."

"I have the feeling that you are always comparing the two of us, that I don't compare to her." I can hear the pain in Siena's voice—the anger of her doubts, and I hate that I have been the cause of it. I know how possessive Elementals can be. If it was me, I would have been losing my shit thinking about Siena having feelings for someone else besides me. Just the thought has my anger rising at a faceless man.

Drawing Siena towards me, I cup her face with my hands, her eyes lifting to mine, and I can see the uncertainty in them.

"I know it was a long time ago, and I know that it's

silly of me to be thinking like this, but you still had her painting."

"Siena, trust me when I say that there is no comparison. I realized the moment I met you, that this between us is completely different from what I could ever have had with any other woman. I didn't want it to be true because she was good to me. I wanted to be able to give her what she wanted, but now that I know what having a mate is like I know that no matter how much I tried, I would never have had the connection with her like I have with you." Moving back a tendril of hair that has slipped over her eyes, I lean down and kiss her lips gently. "If I had to lose you, I know that I would lose my shit and there is nothing or no one that could do anything to stop it, you have become a part of me, my every hour is surrounded with thoughts of you."

I cannot have my woman thinking that I want someone else, even if that someone is dead. "Siena, you are the one I want. You are the only one on my mind and the only one that has ever made me feel the way I do."

A tear slips down her cheek, professing all the hurt that she was feeling. I kiss her again, this time more passionately.

Siena's arms slip around my neck, pulling me closer. My woman has a way about her that makes me feel like I'm the only man in the world. She touches me with a tenderness that humbles me. Her emotions are as clear as day on her face for all to see. I deepen the kiss, taking us on a journey of desire as I lower my arms, grabbing her ass and pulling her up as her legs slide around my waist.

"You, only you," I state before taking both of us on a long exploration of our carnal passions. Siena drives me crazy with lust as she scrapes her nails lightly up my neck, through my hair, never once breaking the kiss. If it takes the rest of our lives, I will make sure that Siena feels the passion that she has awakened in me. She will know that being the mate of an elemental is unique.

Walking towards the bed, I lay her down before me. Sliding my hands under my T-shirt that she's wearing, I pull it up and over her head. Next, I unhook her bra, pulling it off to display her perky breasts for my view. "Take your panties off," I order as I stand back to pull off my jeans, my eyes following her movements.

I am as hard as Thor's hammer, my cock weeping with excitement. When I saw her at the pool, her body on display for the others to see, I saw red. I swear if any of them were unmated, I would have gouged their eyes out but knowing that the others had their women there and were too busy looking at their own women to worry about mine helped.

"Tease," I grunt, as she moves her hands slowly up her legs after disposing of her panties. She runs her fingers up her inner thigh, over her mound, up her flat belly, and stops at her breasts that she fondles as her eyes hold mine. Her fingers tweak the hard nipples, and has my mouth watering at the thought of her taste in my mouth.

Grabbing her ankles, I slide them around my waist as I open her legs and step between them. My hands run up the outside of her legs, over her calves, knees, and thighs. I lean down, my hardened cock sliding over her glistening folds as I take one of her nipples between my lips. My hips moving, thrusting, teasing as I don't penetrate, and instead tease both of us as we rub our bodies against each other. Siena's nails scrape over my back in excitement.

Sucking deeply, I hear her gasp, lifting slightly as I draw her nipple in with my teeth, nibbling at its tenderness as I build an inferno of lust within Siena that has her lifting her chest against my face. My hips rub harder against her sensitive body, creating gasps of pleasure from her and driving my cock to a frantic excitement that has me blind with lust.

My woman is a passionate goddess that can drive the cum from my body in an explosive eagerness that I have never encountered before. I know that if I don't take her soon, I am going to explode like an inexperienced teenager.

Rearing back, I look down at Siena. "You drive me fucking crazy." I grunt just before I join our bodies in a torrent explosion of the senses.

"Ei…" Siena starts to say just before I pull partially out and then thrust in hard, stopping only to hear her gasp. Her eyes glaze over with passion. Their slumberous look inciting my drive to bring her to an earth-shattering explosion of the senses.

I need to hold back. I don't want to hurt her as my thrusts become harder, and her gasps louder as my grunts get deeper. Fuck, nothing can ever be as good as this. I can feel her body start to tremble, her hands grab at my wrists, her nails digging into my flesh as her torso rises and she screams. Her muscles stiffen around me, drawing a deep growl from deep within me as I let go and jet streams of my essence empty inside of her.

Siena can bring life to the dead with her passionate gasps. My heart is racing, and my body is completely drained. My woman is a sex machine, driving me faster to reach the finish line. Leaning down, I take her lips in a deep, gentle kiss. Everything about her fills me with…

There is a bang on the door interrupting my thoughts and this moment. "What?" I snap in anger at the interruption.

"We are riding," Colborn calls out. He does not sound at all sorry for having to interrupt us, the asshole.

I lower my forehead against Siena's. Taking in a deep breath, I slowly expel it to try to calm myself as I gently pull out, feeling her cavern of love tightening around me.

There is another rap on the door. "Hello, anybody there?" I can hear the amusement in Colborn's voice.

"Fuck off!"

His chuckle has me glaring at the door when I hear him walking away.

"Do you have to go?" Looking back at Siena, I nod. I know that Colborn wouldn't have interrupted us if it wasn't necessary. If he says we are riding, it means that something came up that we need to go and check. I'm sure it's those fucking Desperados. I swear we should just kill the sons of bitches and get it over and done with.

"When will you be back?" Siena's slumberous voice has me wanting to say to hell with whatever is going on and lay down beside her.

"I'm not sure. But you rest, and hopefully I will be back before you get out of this bed."

Her smile warms my heart, knowing that she has hopefully been appeased about my marriage and Isabela. Leaning down, I kiss her tenderly before getting up and slipping on a clean T-shirt and jeans. I would rather have showered before going out, but desperate times call for desperate measures.

"Be careful," Siena calls as I head towards the door.

"Of course," I reply, glancing back and freezing as I see her leaning against the headboard, her breasts proudly on display, one leg straight and one slightly bent, but open enough for me to see her passionate folds awaiting my touch.

"Fuck, I'm hard again," I mutter, which has her grinning.

The minx. She did that on purpose. "Tease! You will pay for that," I state as I open the door and slip out the door as she laughs.

"Promise?" I hear her quip just as I close the door. I swear this better be worth it, because if I left my woman to go out for a joy ride, I will not be happy. Making my way outside, I hear the men talking amongst themselves as they await my arrival.

"At last, thought I would have to come and help you put your jeans on," Ulrich teases.

"Shit, bro, you could have showered," Tal states as I walk past him, showing him the finger.

"You were in a hurry so you can put up with my smell. Where the fuck are we going, anyway?"

"We got word on where Basil and his boys are going to be," Tor replies just before he fires up his ride. Fuck, looks like we're going to put an end to this today after all. Adjusting my jeans to try to ease the tightness around my cock, I start my Harley. Whatever is coming for them, they deserve it. Those fuckers are rotten to their core, and nothing will save them now except divine intervention.

Opening up the throttle, I head in the direction where Einar, Garth, and Tor have gone. The others, except for Haldor and Dag, are missing from our group, which tells me that they are staying behind to look after the women. I see that two of our prospects are also riding with us. Tor must be expecting trouble, or he wouldn't have had the prospects join a fight like this.

I'm surprised to see us head out of town. Where are these assholes holed up at? We ride for about forty minutes before Tor is pulling up at a layby. "They should be just up the road at a turn off that leads to a farm on our left." If they are on a farm instead of their usual hangouts in town, that can only mean that they are here for a reason.

"Keep your eyes peeled. I am told that some of those enhanced fuckers are still hanging around with them," Tor warns as he points at Einar and then Tal. "You two, find a spot to park. I want you further up the road in a spot that is hidden, then make your way from that side into the house. Eirik, Garth, and Colborn, you will park your bikes somewhere here and make your way towards the house on foot from here. When the five of you are in place, let us know, and we will ride up to the front door."

Tal and Einar pull away, making their way past the entrance to the house. Colborn, Garth, and I get off our bikes, pushing them into the area surrounded by trees next to the road. We then make our way through the trees in the direction that Tor said their house will be. I feel a tingling race down my spine as we see the house.

Looking around, I try to find any danger that could be imminent, but everything seems quiet—too quiet. "Something feels off," I whisper, as I don't want any of the enhanced fuckers to hear us. Garth and Colborn are also looking around with a suspicious expression. Garth nods. Pulling out his phone, he sends Tor a text.

Before he has a chance to slide the phone back into his pocket, a shot rings out which has the three of us immediately diving to the ground. Hearing a grunt, I look towards Colborn and Garth to see blood starting to gush out of a wound on Garth's shoulder. "Motherfuckers" he roars.

If he hadn't reacted as fast as he did at the sound of the shot, he would now be dead. The question is, how the hell didn't we hear the asshole that shot at us? Colborn raises his hand towards Garth only to have another shot ring out. He snaps his hand back just before the bullet crashes into the ground next to where he's lying.

"Where the fuck is he, can you see him?" I ask as I look around because I can't see where the fucker is hiding. I hear another shot, but this one isn't in the same place or directed at us. "Shit, this is a fucking trap," I mutter.

"They knew we were coming," Garth snaps angrily.

"Who the hell gave Tor this intel?" I ask as I continue searching for any sign of who is shooting at us.

"Drake," Garth replies.

"Our prospect?" Colborn asks which has Garth

grunt and nod. "How the fuck did he get this info?"

"Said one of his contacts told him," Garth's reply has me grunting in anger as I glance behind me only to see a big fucker approaching. How the hell can't we hear them?

"Behind us," I roar as I snap to my feet and run towards him. A shot rings out again but I continue running and swerving left and right as I approach the asshole that is now pointing his gun at me and grinning.

"Die," he says in a soft, emotionless voice just before he pulls the trigger. Shit, it's difficult enough dodging a bullet from behind, but now also from this asshole. I dive to my left and into a bush. I hear Colborn swear as he too makes a dash, but instead of heading towards where we came from, he is heading towards where the shooter is.

I'm about to jump up when I am pulled from where I am and punched with such force that I fly back, hitting a tree and sliding back onto the ground. Shit. I try to catch my breath as the fucker makes his way towards me. This asshole is fast and quiet. Whatever they have done to this guy, he is good. As he leans down to grab me, I throw out my leg, kicking him off his feet.

There will be no holding back from me, as this guy

is more than capable of whipping my ass. I hear a grunt from somewhere, sounding like it might be Garth but I'm not sure as I stand, still trying to catch my breath as I walk towards the fucker that is also standing as if he didn't just get kicked a few feet away, through the air, and crashing onto the ground.

"Who the fuck are you?" I ask, only to receive a sarcastic grin from him as he once again steps towards me. One thing is made abundantly clear, whoever this guy is, he is here to kill, and is not worried about dying in the process.

I smile back at him, starting to enjoy the fight. He is a strong motherfucker, but I am stronger. I wait for him to make his move before I duck when he throws a punch, pulling back my arm as I punch him on his right-side, hearing bones crack under the blow. He grunts but doesn't step back, instead he raises his knee, catching my back.

After that, the fight begins in earnest. These enhanced sons of bitches are strong. Whatever they have been giving them to empower them is working. When he grabs my T-shirt to pull me forward, I let him as I place my hands on his chest as if to hold him back, but instead I envision the water in his body drop down to his legs and feet. I see his shocked look as he stares at me, and then his eyes rolling back as he falls.

"I want to see you do that, asshole." I mutter as I step back. They can enhance their strength and senses and even try to give them some powers, but they will never be able to do what we can.

SIENA 16

My eyes burst open to the sound of a gun firing. My heart starts racing when I think of Eirik being hurt. Jumping off the bed, still naked as when he left me, I hurry to dress in case someone walks in here. I'm looking for my sneakers when I hear another shot, then Anastasia Is screaming, which has me running out of the room with only my T-shirt and jeans on.

"What's going on?" I ask when I see Esmeralda hurrying towards the bar area.

"From what I can hear, it's the Desperados trying to breach the gate, but Dag and Haldor are there holding them back with two of the prospects, I think Drake and…

I gasp in fright. Before Esmeralda can finish her sentence there is a loud cracking sound and then we see two men that are clearly not bikers rushing towards us. "Oh no, you don't," I scream as I hold out my hands. I draw the current in, feeling it flow through my body and then I am letting it out through my hands just as the men come close enough to try to grab us.

When the current hits one of the men he is thrown

back against the wall, the other screams in pain, and then he is falling where he was standing. I breathe in slowly, still feeling the current flowing through my body. I can feel its force stronger than I have ever felt it before and realize by the men's unconscious states that my power has in fact grown since bonding with Eirik.

"Oh, my word. I was sure that we were done for when I saw those two guys coming for us, but damn, Siena," Esmeralda says in awe as she looks at me. "You literally toasted their ass." Just then Anastasia and Freya come running from inside the bar area with a worried expression on their faces as they stop dead in their tracks when they see the two men.

"What happened here?" Freya asks in surprise as she looks at the men.

"They came in through the back. I think they broke in through the back door," Esmeralda explains as we hear more gunfire. "What is happening outside?"

"We went out to help Dag and Haldor, and I swear they nearly had a mini heart attack," Anastasia replies grumpily. "There are a few men on the outside of the gate, but it seems like our men are holding them back fine, so we decided to come inside. After all, why should we be disturbing their enjoyment?"

"Besides, it looks like we might be needed here," Freya states as she looks around. "I think we should tie these two up."

"I don't think they are going anywhere in a hurry," Esmeralda says as she shakes her head and points at me. "You two should have seen this one. She's lethal. Sparks actually fly out of her hands."

"That's so cool," Anastasia says as she walks towards the man that hit the wall. "I might need your services sometime to shock some sense into my man's thick skull." I smile at her quip as she pokes the man with the tip of her foot. "Yeah, I think this one is out cold."

"I will go and find something to tie their hands," Freya says as she hurries away.

"We can use this on one of them," Esmeralda suggests as she pulls a long burgundy scarf from where she has it around her extended waist, like a belt.

"No, don't go near them," I warn as I take the scarf from her. "If they wake up while we are tying them up, I don't want them to hurt you." I see her smile as I turn with the scarf in my hand towards the closest guy that is sprawled a few feet away.

Leaning down, I pull his arm around his back, and then try to turn him to bring the other arm around, Anastasia comes to help, but the minute she touches him she jumps back with a gasp as she feels a slight discharge of energy from him. "Umm, I don't think it's safe to touch them." I laugh at her raised brows.

"Don't worry, it does nothing to me," I assure her as I finally manage to bring his arm back. I stand to go to the other one as Freya comes rushing towards us with a pair of handcuffs in her hands. "Well, I never took you for the kinky type," I tease, as she hands me the handcuffs.

"Oh, they're not mine," she says hurriedly. "I heard one of the Jezebels talking the other day about her sexual toys and how she would just once like to get Tor into handcuffs, but apparently he doesn't want to. Seeing all three of them are out today, I thought they wouldn't mind if I borrowed them." Freya's sweet tone has me grinning as I shake my head, taking the cuffs just as Dag rushes in.

His eyes find Esmeralda, they run over her body to make sure that she is fine before turning to the men on the ground. "Did these assholes touch any of you?"

"No. Siena stopped them in their tracks," Esmeralda says, which has Dag looking at me and then his eyebrow rises when he sees the handcuffs in my hands.

"Never took Eirik for a submissive," he states.

"Oh no, this isn't mine," I say quickly before he thinks that Eirik is being handcuffed to the bed. the thought has me wanting to laugh. "Freya brought them so we can handcuff that one."

At my confession, his head snaps towards Freya. "Dane?" he asks, his expression one of complete surprise as he thinks about Dane using the handcuffs.

"No, Dag. The handcuffs are one of the Jezebels and apparently she uses them on Tor," Anastasia says with a sweet smile.

"What?" his roar of surprise is so funny to see that we all start laughing at his complete astonishment.

"You are joking, right?" he asks, uncertain.

"Nope," Anastasia says, a grin spread across her face.

"Fuck me, I would never have thought," Dag mutters as he walks towards the guy against the wall that is starting to rouse. I see Freya shaking her head at Anastasia's prank and Anastasia shrug innocently.

"Oh, be careful whe…" I start to warn but it's too late as Dag places his hand on his arm, a pulse of current rushes through him which has his hand snapping back and his head turning to look at me.

"Did you zap them?" he asks.

"A little zap," I say, which has Esmeralda elbow me.

"Little?" she asks.

"Okay, maybe medium." He leans towards the guy again, this time touching him carefully. I notice his muscles flex as he feels the current, but he doesn't jump back again, and instead places the handcuffs on the guy.

"I hope Tor doesn't get upset that the guy is using his handcuffs," Anastasia says innocently, which has me holding back a laugh as Dag looks at her in aghast.

"Tor," he says the name while shaking his head, as if he can't believe it. "Fuck me!" he mutters.

"Looks like they're all gone," Haldor says as he walks in. His eyes roaming around the room to see what damage is before he takes in the two men. "Except these two that is, and the dead ones outside."

"Wait, there are dead men outside?" Anastasia asks, horrified. A reaction that I am also feeling, and going by Freya and Esmeralda's expressions, so are they.

"Well… umm…" Haldor starts to say, as he looks at a scowling Dag. "They might be unconscious."

I want to laugh at his uncomfortable expression but then shake my head when I realize that just a couple of months ago, I would have been horrified at everything that has happened today, but instead, I zapped two guys that were trying to hurt us, and now I want to laugh at the fact that Haldor is uncomfortable over the fact that there are dead men in the front of the club and he doesn't know how to lie about it to us.

"We need to go and scout the property. If these two assholes got in, there might be more about," Dag says.

"How did they know to come here today when the others aren't here?" Haldor asks with a frown. "I think that is very convenient for them, isn't it?"

"Yeah. But we will have to think about that later," Dag says and then looks at us. "I want you all to go into Tor's room and stay there until we come and get you."

"Why Tor's room?" Freya asks.

"That room is bomb proof. Trust me. Go in there and lock the door," he replies as he approaches Esmeralda, placing a hand on her cheek. I see him looking deep into her eyes before he lowers his head and kisses her lightly on the lips. "You, okay?"

She nods.

"Okay then. Go on, we will leave once you are all inside his room," he orders as he steps back from his mate.

"You do know that we can protect ourselves, don't you?" Anastasia grumbles as she starts making her way towards Tor's room. I follow the others, closing the door behind me and locking it when the four of us are inside and then freeze when I look around. I shut my mouth realizing that I am standing here like a fish out of water staring at his room.

"What the hell is that?" I ask, looking at a weird contraption, which I'm not sure is for pleasure or pain.

"I wouldn't ask If I was you. Knowing Tor, it will be worse than we can possibly imagine," Freya replies as she goes to sit on his massive bed.

"He really takes the whole Viking theme seriously, doesn't he?" I state as I approach the others that are making themselves comfortable. The pelts on the floor. The massive bed with the handcrafted legs and headboard. Entering his room feels like I have just gone back in time and found myself in a Viking's lair.

"You have no idea," Anastasia says. "Even the parties are raunchy."

"You know, I have always been curious about his room when I heard the two of you talking," Esmeralda mentions as she looks around and then laughs when her eyes fall on a painting of a naked woman. "This one is worse than the one behind his desk in the office," she states.

"I wonder who the woman is? It's the same one." Freya's words have me looking at the painting and the woman's face.

"You know, I never realized that," Anastasia replies as she walks towards the painting, coming to a halt before it as she looks at it closely. "I think because our eyes are drawn to other parts of her, we miss her face."

I laugh. I haven't seen the painting in Tor's office, but if it's anything like this one, I can see why Anastasia would say that as the first thing that draws our eyes is her bountiful breasts, then down to her hand that does very little to hide her mound. Her long raven black hair is flowing around her, her clear green eyes slumberous looking, as if she has just been made love to thoroughly. Her skin is tanned and looks as smooth as silk.

"She's stunning when you actually get to look at her face," Anastasia says as she continues to look at the painting. "I wonder who painted this? They captured her beautifully."

"He must have had something going on with her at some time. After all, he has two paintings of the same woman," Esmeralda says.

"Looks like they all like keeping paintings of their memories, doesn't it?" I say sarcastically, thinking of the painting Eirik had at the head of his bed.

"You know, I don't think this is a painting from the past." Anastasia lifts her hand, pointing towards the side table next to the woman. "That's a phone, unless they were making cell phones when the Vikings were around, I think this is quite current." The woman in the painting has a braid on each side of her face and a gold bracelet like the ones Tor uses on her arm, but Anastasia is right. This woman isn't from his past.

"Do you think she is someone he knows?" Freya

asks, with a curious expression on her face.

"Must be. He does have two paintings of her, unless he just likes this artist's work," Anastasia suggests as she raises on her tiptoes to try to see something. "Esmeralda, can you see an artist's name on here?"

Esmeralda can use her abilities to see better than anyone here I look at her as she looks at the painting, her eyes roving over it.

She shakes her head. "Nope."

Freya gets up, walking towards the painting to stand next to Anastasia. "That's strange, usually artists sign their work," she says.

"Maybe it's on the back?" I suggest.

"You think?" Freya asks, as she glances back at me.

"I don't know, as it's a raunchy painting maybe the artist didn't want people to know who painted it," I reply with a shrug.

Anastasia turns, heading towards a big throne-like chair placed by the window. I laugh when she takes hold of the back, trying to move it but it doesn't budge.

"Jeepers, is this thing made of steel or what?" she mutters as she tries again, huffing when she simply moves it half a foot.

"Maybe gold," Esmeralda quips, also grinning at her efforts.

"Well, some help would be great!" she states as she places her hands on her hips and she looks at us. "You do want to know who painted that, don't you?"

"Not really," Esmeralda teases.

"We could contact the artist and find out who the woman is," Freya suggests as she walks to help Anastasia.

"You just sit," I order Esmeralda as she moves to stand. "You don't want to be pulling and picking stuff up in your condition." I hear her sigh as I come to stand next to Anastasia.

"I'm not an invalid," she argues.

"Of course not, honey, just pregnant," Freya confirms as we start pushing the chair towards the painting. Anastasia wasn't joking, it is heavy. "Why the hell does he want such a heavy and ugly chair in this room,"

"It's his throne," I grunt as we push it the last couple of feet.

"He probably does see it as such. I'm surprised he doesn't have it in the bar area and makes us all bow to him," Anastasia quips with a laugh as she stands on the chair, leaning towards the painting. She lifts the bottom to look behind it.

"Don't give him any ideas. He probably would," Freya laughs.

"There is nothing here either." Anastasia mutters as she lifts it a little more.

"Let me look," Esmeralda says, coming to stand against the wall as she looks up behind the painting. "Can't see anything."

"Strange, why would someone not sign their name when they are clearly talented," I ask.

"Do you think maybe he painted it?" Anastasia asks as she looks down at us.

"No," Esmeralda replies with a frown. "I can't see him holding a paintbrush. A gun, axe, or even sword, yes, but a paintbrush no."

"Esmeralda is right," Freya agrees. "Tor is way too rough to be a painter."

"Then who painted this?" Anastasia asks as she steps down from the chair, "because it must have been someone he knows."

"Maybe it's the woman in the painting." I suggest, as I look up at the painting.

"Now I really want to know who she is," Anastasia agrees. "Shall we have a snoop around?"

"Knowing Tor, he will know and have our heads," Freya retorts.

"We should put the chair back in its place first," I advise.

"Someone is coming," Esmeralda interrupts as we start to push the chair back into place.

"Damn," Anastasia mutters as she quickly takes a seat in it just as the handle on the door rattles.

"Who is it?" Freya asks, which has the person on the other side stop trying to open the door. We wait, but there is no reply.

"The person is going away," Esmeralda whispers, which has us all looking at each other in surprise. Why would one of our guys not reply and just leave?

"Tha…" Anastasia starts to say, but Esmeralda lifts her hand for silence. Looking at her, we wait to see what she says. We wait in silence as she listens to what is happening outside. A few minutes later she shrugs. "The person went outside but they haven't spoken to anyone, I don't know who it was."

"Strange, don't you think?" my question has the others nod, something doesn't feel right.

EIRIK 17

"Didn't you find him?" Tor asks as Colborn and Einar approach. When the fighting began, we all got separated, but after disposing of the guys that came at us, we realized that one of ours was missing. These fuckers were waiting for us. This was an ambush.

"No, there is no sign of him," Einar mutters as he comes to stand before Tor and me. His hands are low on his waist as he stands with us, waiting for the others to come back. Tor sent us all out to check the area for any sign of Tal. We know that he isn't dead, or we would have found evidence of his death and felt the shift in energy.

"Those motherfuckers must have him," I grunt in anger, thinking of what they will subject him to.

"We will wait for the others to make sure," Tor replies, the anger vibrating in his voice. "Someone will catch the vibration of his energy."

"We fucking better," Colborn growls in anger as he paces before us. His furious energy crackling around him as he steps. "Those enhanced sons of bitches are starting to piss me off."

Just then Garth and Dane come into view as Ulrich and Asgar approaching from the other side.

"Nothing," Ulrich states as he comes to a stop a few feet away, throwing up his hands "This is not good."

Garth shakes his head when he gets to us.

"There must be some sign of him. We will all go back in and comb that fucking property until we find something," Tor roars as he heads towards the edge of the property. "Spread out," he orders.

We won't leave Tal behind They took him, but we will find him. The anger coursing through my veins is like a live wire of fury that wants a target to be unleashed on. I start walking back towards the house, moving through the wooded area slowly as not to miss anything. The closer we get to the house, the angrier I get when I don't find any signs of Tal.

There was something off from the minute we walked into this fucking property. There is something that we are not seeing. I take another step and freeze. "Where did they come from?"

My question has the others stop their search.

"There is no way that they were here, or we would have sensed them. Do they have something masking their energy, or did they just appear? Which I don't think is possible unless they're ghosts."

"Trust me, the two bastards I fought were real," Asgar calls.

"So, how did they appear without us hearing or seeing them?" I ask.

"Fuck me," Dane suddenly grunts. The next minute he is lifting his hands above his head and closing his eyes as if to bend the air around him. "They dropped in," he states suddenly as he turns towards where Tor is standing with a scowl adorning his face. "The ones that left must have done it the same way."

"Shit, how are we going to find him like that?" Ulrich asks, throwing his hands up.

"We can ask Draco. Maybe Jasmine or Gabriela will be able to see something," Einar replies with a raised brow.

"We could also get Zane." I know that there will be opposition in asking Zane to help us. After all, Zane can't be trusted most of the time because he is unpredictable. The guy is out of his rocker most of the time, but he's our best bet when it comes to tracking in the air.

"Yeah, and how the hell are you going to do that?"

Colborn asks. "The asshole is a force unto himself and listens to no one. You know Draco would give us hell if we were to deal with him."

"I will speak to Draco about Jasmine helping us, and then I will find Zane and bring him here by his fucking balls if I have to. But if he can help us, then he will help," Tor states as he looks at us, his energy palpable with the rage he is holding at bay.

"Fuck, Tor, are you sure?" Einar asks. "That asshole is a loose cannon."

"He might be a loose cannon, but he has mastered his element like no one ever has," Tor replies. "I will make sure that he finds Tal." With those words Tor snaps around, making his way back towards where we have our bikes.

"That was not a good suggestion," Einar remarks as he walks past. Einar and Zane have history. But that is something that we will all have to live with if he can somehow find Tal. When we reach the bikes, Tor is on his phone, his body tense as he talks. The grave tone of his voice has all of us making a beeline for our Harley's.

It's not a good idea to be around Tor when he loses his shit, but rather clear a path and let him be. We are all revved up from the fight, and now that they have taken Tal, our tempers are crackling. "Son of a bitch," Tor roars and then his phone is being thrown. Shit, he's not going to be too happy about that when he calms down.

Whatever Draco had to say did not make him happier. "They attacked the club while we were gone." Those words have me snapping to attention. He wasn't talking to Draco; he must have been talking to one of the guys at our club.

"What happened?" If they touched Siena, I will hunt every single one of them down and skin them. I lean forward, starting my bike as he confirms that the women are fine. I notice Ulrich is already revving his bike, riding towards home like a bat out of hell. I don't blame him; all I want to do is make sure that Siena is fine. I want to see her with my own eyes.

This whole day was a cluster fuck. We got duped into coming here, which resulted in Tal going missing, and they took that opportunity to penetrate our club. Motherfuckers need to die. I twist the throttle, letting the bike race me back home. Ulrich is just before me and I can hear the others behind, but I don't pay anyone any attention as I ride around the twisty bends.

At any other time, I would have enjoyed this ride, but today I am driven to reach Siena as soon as possible. I do not like the fact that I wasn't there when she needed me. I don't like this danger that we live, this danger that constantly follows us.

The drum from the motor beats through my body like the staccato changing of the gears until I am one with my ride. The wind blowing around me until it feels like there is no one around but me. My thoughts are on Siena and the trauma that she has gone through. It's unfair that evil has touched her so often, all because she is my mate.

I slide to a halt before the club. Jumping off my bike as I make my way inside, I see the two prospects near the entrance washing a stain of blood on the ground, but I don't stop to ask questions. There will be enough time for that later For now, I just need to see my woman—feel her and make sure that she is fine.

My instinct guides me, taking me to Tor's room. It makes sense that they be in here since it's the safest room in the club. Tor's room is like a safe room. There won't be any human that can enter the room unless they know the location of the tunnel. But through all these years that we have been living here, it hasn't been breached, and no one knows about the tunnel except some of the brothers.

Just as I am about to bang on the door, the handle turns, and it shoots open. Ulrich is stepping in and pulling Anastasia into a bear hug before she realizes what is happening.

"Eirik!"

Siena's gasp of surprise when she sees me is the best sound I could ever have heard. Reaching for her, I pull her hard against me. Her arms snap around my neck as I lower my head to take her lips in a blistering kiss.

I sense the others moving around, but I don't break this hypnotic moment with my woman until a few minutes later when she reluctantly pulls back. "You're back," she whispers as her hand moves down over my neck, to my chest and my stomach.

"Are you okay?" I ask, looking deeply into her eyes to see her reaction. A slow smile spreads across her face as she looks back at me.

"I am now," she whispers. "Are you all back?"

Her question has my mind going back to the fact that Tal is missing. "No, Tal is missing."

My statement has her gasping and her body tensing. "What happened?"

At any other time I would have sidestepped this question to not upset her, but they attacked the club too. They could have harmed any one of the women. It is time that everyone be aware of what is happening and keep safe. Therefore, I find myself relating the events of earlier today to her, which have her gasping, her eyes widening, when I explain that we were ambushed and that we think this was a setup.

"Someone came and tried the door earlier," Siena mentions when I am finished. "We all thought it was really strange because they did not answer when we asked who was there."

Her revelation has me tensing as I glance over my shoulder at Ulrich, that is hugging his woman close. I see that Esmeralda and Freya have left while we were hugging, probably telling their men what happened.

"Maybe just one of the guys making sure that you were all safe, but we will find out who it was so that we can calm your mind," I promise, also wanting to know who would have come to Tor's room just as we are attacked.

"Fuck, did they touch any of you?" I hear Ulrich's rumble.

"No, they came in through the back, but little did they know that we have our very own taser in the house." Anastasia's words have me frowning and by Ulrich's question I'm guessing him too.

"Taser?"

"Yeah, Siena put them down. When Dag went to tie them up, they were still letting out current." I look back at Siena, only to see her smiling at Anastasia as she shakes her head in amusement.

"You shocked them?" I ask, looking over her body again to make sure that she is fine.

"Well, they were coming directly at Esmeralda and I, and there was no one else around." Her eyes are intense now as she looks at me. "I am never going to let someone else take me against my will if I can help it."

"I'm sorry I wasn't here," I say as I pull her close again. I hate the fact that she had to defend herself and that I wasn't here to protect her.

"So, we have two prisoners that you caught?" Ulrich states, shaking his head, which has Anastasia slapping his stomach lightly.

"See, we aren't powerless after all," she quips.

"Baby, I never thought you were powerless, I have evidence that you can freeze someone right to their bones." What Ulrich says is true, Anastasia has one wicked gift of freezing whatever she wants. When I first saw her doing it, I was impressed to see how effortlessly she can freeze an area solid.

"Except you," she murmurs with a shrug.

"Baby, you stiffen my bone all the time," he jokes, which has her slapping his stomach again and laughing.

"You perv, shhh," she whispers.

"Will you help us push that chair back into place?" Siena asks, suddenly pointing at Tor's throne, looking at the scuff marks on the floor I'm surprised to see that the women moved it.

"Why were you moving his throne?" I ask with a raised brow.

"His throne?" Siena asks surprised, "so it really is supposed to be a throne?"

I nod as I let go of her to go and pick up the solid chair and take it back to where I know it usually should be.

"Should I even ask why you were moving that?"

"Umm," Siena starts and then looks at Anastasia with uncertainty.

"We were just trying to see his painting more closely," Anastasia replies with a shrug, a reply that has my brow raising in question.

"You couldn't see it from the ground?" Ulrich also

questions as he looks at the painting.

"It doesn't have a painter's name; do you know that?" Anastasia reveals as she points at the painting.

I look over at it, seeing the contours of the naked woman, the same naked woman that Tor has hanging behind his desk in the office. "No, it wouldn't," I mutter as I place my arm around Siena's shoulders, guiding her out of the room because I suddenly feel like an intruder.

Tor is secretive about his life. Even though I have known him for centuries, I still don't know the whole truth about his background. The only one that knows more about Tor than I do is Draco, and I know that the story about this woman in the painting is one of Tor's secrets that he would rather not anyone know.

I know enough to keep my mouth shut, know enough to respect his secrets.

SIENA 18

Yesterday was madness. I never thought I'd go through something like that. But ever since I was kidnapped, my life has changed completely. My normal, boring life is now filled with danger and excitement. I used to complain about how my life was always the same thing. Well, I'm sure I am being punished now for complaining, because I don't think anyone has a hundred- and eighty-degree change like I have.

The frustrated woman that constantly dreamt of a different life is now mated to a man that any woman would gladly sleep with. His looks are a wet dream waiting to happen. Even the light scar he has on his face adds to his magnetism. When I first asked him about the scar, he was reluctant to reveal its origin, but then he told me that when his wife died, her father was beside himself with the fact that Eirik couldn't help her. He didn't go into detail, but he mentioned that he tried to kill him, and because of his feelings of guilt in not being able to give her what a true mate should have, he made sure that the scar didn't heal and stayed evident for him to remember what he did.

Looking towards where the men are, I shake my head, still bemused at how I got here. The room is filled with dangerous looking men—men whose tempers are running rampant. This morning Draco, Wulf, Ceric, Burkhart and Bjarni arrived, and I still can't stop looking at them.

The absolute animalistic quality in all of them is hypnotic. When Wulf caught my eye earlier, I swear he was looking right into my soul, his violet-coloured eyes mesmerizing. "So, girl, I hear you can give guys a bit of a shock?" Looking towards Nova, who is leaning against the counter in the bar, I smile. Meeting some of these women has been fun. I'm still amazed at how there are so many women out there with such amazing gifts, and the world doesn't know about how many special people there are in the world.

"You could say that," I reply with a shrug.

"Don't be modest, Siena, you nearly fried their asses," Anastasia interrupts.

"Now that is an interesting gift to have. I wouldn't mind shocking Ceric every now and again," Nova states as she looks over at her man that is bent over one of the tables, looking at a drawing of the area where Tal went missing.

"I think you do enough of that on a daily basis,

don't you?" Gabriela asks from where she's looking down at her phone texting.

"Yeah, but just think," Nova says. "When we're both in bed and he's about to go to sleep, I shock him just a little to get his blood pumping, or when he's being irritating I shock him enough to curl his hair."

At her words, I laugh, shaking my head. The others warned me about Nova and how crazy she can be.

"The only problem is that I can't shock any of the Elementals." I see Nova's eyes widen at my statement and then a grin widens across her face.

"You don't know?" There is a naughty grin on her face as she looks at the other women. "You didn't tell her?"

"Tell her what?" Freya asks with a frown.

"No!" Nova says in surprise. "Are you telling me that they are keeping this a secret from you guys?"

"Keeping what a secret?" Anastasia asks.

"Nova, Tor isn't going to be pleased with you," Jasmine says from where she's sitting next to Gabriela.

"Really? And what's he going to do, ban me from

coming here?" she asks, with a mischievous expression on her face. "Oh wait, he already did that, and guess what?" She twirls around. "Here I am."

"What secret?" Anastasia asks again.

"We can all use our gifts with the Elementals. The only trick is that you need to be touching another of the women while touching the Elemental for it to work."

Her statement has me looking at Esmeralda, who is frowning at Nova, and then back to Nova.

"Are you saying that if I want to shock someone, I would just need to hold your hand, for example, and touch the Elemental, and I would be able to shock them?"

Nova smiles as she nods.

"You want to try it?"

"Nova!" Katrina calls in a warning as she shakes her head in amusement. "You're going to get her into trouble."

"Nonsense, they need to know," she replies.

"That means I can freeze Ulrich when he's being a real ass." Anastasia says with a big grin on her face.

"Oh, Nova, this is great news."

"The guys won't think so," Gabriela quips with a wink just as we hear a deep snarl that has all of us turning towards the group of men to see Draco and Tor facing each other in anger.

"I said no," Draco states in a low, angry voice.

"If he can help us find Tal, I am getting him," Tor replies, his voice also vibrating in anger

"The only thing he will find is trouble. There is no controlling him," Draco warns in a low intense tone.

"I am not leaving him out there if there is the smallest chance that Zane can find him," Tor replies, stepping back and throwing his hands up in frustration.

"Jasmine saw him in a cell. We just need to figure out where," Wulf interrupts in a quiet voice. When they arrived earlier, they mentioned that Jasmine had a vision of Tal and that he was being held in a cell. At least that gave everyone hope that he was still fine and that we had a chance of getting to him before they hurt him, or worse, killed him.

"Unless she saw an address it doesn't help us find him, now does it?" Tor grunts.

"Fuck, Tor, you're one stubborn son of a bitch,"

Draco grunts angrily. "Fine get him, but don't come and complain to me when he spirals out of control, pulling you with him."

Tor grunts as he turns, heading for the exterior door of the club. "Go with him!" Draco inclines his head towards where Tor disappeared as he looks at Colborn and Burkhart just as Garth and Bjarni enter from the back.

"Where the hell did you get those handcuffs from, Bro?" Garth asks as he looks at Dag.

"I didn't, Freya brought them to me," Dag replies, which has Garth's head snapping towards Dane with a surprised look.

"No way, does your woman use those on you?"

His question has Dane snap to attention, his muscles looking as hard as steel. "Fuck off," he grates with a scowl.

"Well, your woman was the one that got them."

Dane looks over his shoulder at Freya with a raised brow.

"Umm," Freya starts, but is interrupted by Anastasia.

"They Tor's." Her words have all the men looking

at her with different expressions on their face. Some of them look shocked, others amused.

"Well, fuck that... Tor has kink in him that he's hiding from all of us," Ceric quips. "Maybe we should get him a blow-up doll like we did Draco?"

"No way. I can't see Tor with handcuffs on, no matter the situation," Eirik states as he shakes his head.

"Come on, boys," Nova interrupts as she takes my hand, pulling me with her. I stand, following her reluctantly. "Everyone has a right to play anyway they like."

"You have been with Ceric for too long, it's clear that he has corrupted you," Asgar says with a smile.

"Ceric corrupted me?" Nova asks as she looks at her mate with a naughty smile. "No, I think it's the other way around." When we come to stand near the men, Eirik comes to stand next to me, sliding his arm around my shoulders.

I see Draco's eyes looking at us suspiciously.

Nova squeezes my hand, which has me glancing at her only to see her inclining her head slightly to Eirik. What? and then I realize what she's asking, she wants me to shock him. I shake my head, which has her frown. "What are you up to?" Ceric suddenly asks as he comes to stand behind his mate, sliding his arms around her waist. "Be good, Nova."

"What?" she says innocently, which has him grunting as he lowers his head and nips her neck.

"Behave," I hear him mutter. Now I know what I can and cannot do, it's nice to know that if I have to use my gift with an Elemental, I can if another woman is around. But I will not be using it against Eirik, at least not right now.

"Where's the prospect that gave Tor the information?" Draco asks.

"Drake is doing the rounds today; do you want me to go and call him?" Asgar asks with a raised brow.

"Yeah."

Asgar nods and walks outside to do Draco's bidding.

Eirik leans down to kiss my neck, his fingers stroking my chin. "Hey, Siena, I hear you zapped the guys that are locked up," Bjarni, one of Draco's men and a giant at that, asks. He and Garth are like two walls standing there.

"They were coming at us. It was either that or let them do whatever they were thinking of doing."

My reply has him nodding, a grin appearing on his face. "It must have been some zapping. The one guy is still incoherent and there is a burn mark where you touched him."

At his words, I shake my head. "I didn't touch them."

My reply has his eyebrows raising.

"You shocked them without touching?"

I nod and he whistles. "Damn, girl, that's some fine moves you have."

"When I went to tie them up, they were still sparking," Dag inputs just as Asgar and Drake walk in. I sense the tension building as the men look at Drake. From what Eirik told me, it was Drake that gave Tor the information about where the Desperados were going to be. It was his fault that they were drawn into a trap. It was his fault that Tal had been taken. Looking at Drake, I see a man with dark brown hair and deep blue eyes looking around nervously as he walks next to Asgar.

"I hear that you got information that wasn't all that we expected. You want to tell me where it came from?" Wulf asks as he leans against one of the tables looking relaxed, but something tells me that it's all a farce, and is anything but relaxed.

"One of the girls I see," Drake replies with a shrug.

"How did this girl know about the information you gave us?" Wulf asks.

"She's friends with some of the Desperados, said they tell her stuff."

"You trusted a woman that is friends with the Desperados to give you information that will get them caught?" Eirik asks with a raised brow.

Drake shrugs. "She seemed genuine, and I have known her for a while."

"Aria?" Draco calls

"He loves this girl, and even though he was suspicious of her information, he believes she wouldn't lie to him."

Draco's eyes are a magnetic blue that just looking at him has chills racing up my spine. I wouldn't like to be in Drake's shoes right now.

"So," Draco says. "You place the whole club's lives in danger because you believed this woman wouldn't lie to you."

"She didn't lie," Drake says with conviction.

"How the fuck do you know that? Is she your mate?" Draco suddenly roars, which has Drake jumping in surprise.

"She's, his sister," Aria says from behind us, which has Drake's eyes snap towards her in surprise. Aria's mind reading is amazing, I never thought that there really were people that could genuinely mind read, but it seems like I was very wrong.

"I want to talk to her!" Draco's statement has Drake tensing.

"She didn't do anything wrong," he replies with conviction. "There must be another explanation."

"Asgar, go with Drake and bring his sister here," Draco orders as he turns his back on Drake, ending their conversation. I can see why everyone has so much respect for Draco. It's evident that he isn't someone to take lightly, his energy radiates authority. I just hope that this sister of Drake will help us in some way to find Tal.

EIRIK 19

Tempers are starting to fray. It has been a week since Tal went missing, and we still haven't found any trace of where Tal is which is messing with everyone. Tal is one of us, a brother that has stood by each one of us when we needed it most, and we will not rest until we find where he is and bring him back.

We have interrogated Drake's sister to no avail, as it seems that she was telling the truth, or she thinks she was. Maybe they gave her that information, knowing that she would tell Drake and he would tell us. Today Zane is meant to arrive, and everyone is on tenterhooks as it has been two centuries since we last saw him.

Tor took a while to find him and then convince him to help us or threaten him to help us, which I think is more the case. Either way, he should be arriving today, and I can tell by Einar's expression that he is not looking forward to it, as Zane and him have history.

Whatever happens, we need to try to hold our opinions and tempers in check until this is over, and we have Tal back home. The one thing that keeps us all going and from losing our shit is the fact that Tal is still alive.

We thought that maybe the Desperados would try to trade Tal's life for Esmeralda's, but there has been no communication from them which tells us that it's not them that have Tal. We suspect that Aldor has Tal somewhere, but with all the money and means he has, there's no way that we will be able to find him soon.

All I know is that whatever happens, we won't give up. We will turn every stone until we find where they have stashed him, and then we will burn the fucking place down. I look up when I sense Siena approaching. With everything that has happened to her, and with the things that are currently going on with the club, I am proud of the way she is holding on.

My woman has got courage. She stood up to those fuckers that were about to attack her and Esmeralda instead of shying away, like most would have done. She has completely drawn me in. I know that she's my mate, and that we were immediately drawn to each other, but nothing would make me love her the way I do if I didn't respect her courage, her wisdom, and her caring nature.

Siena has brought hope and love back into my life.

She has ignited a drive in me that has been dead for a long time. I was ready to give up—ready to find peace instead of the constant fight against myself. Now when I look at myself, I am like a different person, as I know that Siena cares for me. To know that you have someone that genuinely cares and wants you is a feeling that no one can explain. My woman looks at me with such tenderness and love that it ignites the fire in my soul, the water in my body, the light in my mind, and the fervent heat in my heart. I want to live and share myself with her.

I want to show her the world; I want to have a family with her, something that I had given up hope on imagining that I would never be able to see my child looking at me with innocence in its gaze. That I would never be the one to teach my child what I know, to hold a replica of Siena in my arms and know that it was made with love. The love that I hold for its mother.

"Are you hiding in here?"

I smile at her words. "You could say that," I reply as I throw down the cloth I was cleaning my hands with. We will be going out later again, but we have started to believe that Tal isn't in South Africa anymore, and that we need to start looking beyond our borders. When yet another argument broke out between Einar and Burkhart, I decided it was time to leave. Tinkering with my Harley has always kept me busy and out of trouble. It was either that or making love to my woman, but after last night's marathon, I think she will be a little tender. This whole business with Tal is messing with my head and the only way to forget, even if for an hour, is when I am making love to Siena.

Last night was a long session of torrid sexual experiences for her, which exhausted her to the point of not even hearing me get up and showering this morning.

"I didn't take you for a chicken," she teases.

"If I can prevent being part of an argument, I will. Besides, it's much more relaxing than just me and my ride," I tease with a wink.

"Do you have any leads?" she asks with a frown as she comes to stand before me, her hair a flame of radiance flowing around her shoulders, her eyes watchful.

"No, but Zane is arriving today, which will hopefully help us find some kind of vestige of Tal's energy," I reply as I raise my hand to slide it around the back of her neck, massaging the tense muscles there.

"Why don't the guys like Zane?"

Her question has me sighing. "Zane is actually a really good guy, but he doesn't follow rules too well."

"You mean, more than you guys?"

I grin as I shrug, it's true that our chapter isn't much into following rules, but when it comes to Zane, he is a force unto himself.

"The last time Zane was a MC member, he nearly got a few of the others killed because of his rebellious ways, and all because he wanted to show Draco that he could do it," I state, remembering the touch and go situation that got him banned.

"So, Draco and Zane don't like each other," she says, inclining her head.

"I don't know about that. Zane is Draco's younger brother."

She gasps, her eyes widening.

"I think that it's not easy to grow up in Draco's shadow. In my opinion, Zane has always just been trying to measure up to him."

"The girls were saying that Draco is the only one that can bend all the elements. Is that true or can Zane also do it?"

I frown. It's true that Draco is crazy powerful, but I'm sure there are some of us out there that can bend more than one element. Like Tor, for example, he can bend two.

"No. I doubt Zane is anywhere near as powerful as Draco. Firstly, Draco is nearly nine hundred years old, which as you know with time our powers grow. It is true that Draco's ancestors were some of our strongest warriors, his bloodline is pure, same as Zane's, but Draco is older, and until the last time I saw Zane, much wiser."

Siena raises her arms, sliding her hands around my neck. Her breasts rub against my chest, her fragrance enticing my passion.

"All of this still sounds crazy. I can't believe that I am part of a species that is so much more superior than humans, and that we don't even know that you exist."

I lower my head after she speaks and kiss her luscious lips.

"You are now an Elemental, too. We don't want the humans to know that we exist. We blend in as much as we can. Unfortunately, we come with our own wars that sometimes pull humans into the fight without us wanting it." The softness of her body is triggering a reaction that I thought after last night would be dormant for a couple more hours. But I should have known that when it comes to my mate, my body is always ready to respond.

"How are you feeling this morning?" Her eyes rise from my lips to my eyes as a smile spreads across her face.

"A little tender, but I feel like I have more energy than I have ever had before." Her fingers start to massage the back of my neck, her eyes soft with passion. "I can still feel you deep inside me." Her whispered words create an instant reaction. My cock is hard and twitching, wanting to break its restraints.

"Fuck, woman, you have me hard with a simple word." Lowering my hands, I grab her ass, lifting her up slowly so that her pussy rubs against the bulge in my jeans. The movement has both of us groaning. Her legs slide around my waist, our clothes the only barrier stopping us from enjoying this moment fully. Our lips lock in a torrent kiss of lust and complete abandon.

Siena is the balm to this craziness that is happening around us. She is the light that will guide my way as I fight to find Tal. We are all hoping to find him as soon as possible, because each day that passes is one more day that we are letting him down. We are interrupted by the sound of Harley's approaching.

One of them belongs to Tor as I know the sound of his pipes. That means that the other must be Zane.

Lifting my head, I look at Siena's passionate expression, wishing that I could take her back into our room and finish what we just began. But now that Zane is here, we are going to be going out as soon as he gets a trace on Tal's energy.

"Tor and Zane are here," I state as I unlock Siena's legs from behind me and help her stand, guiding her into the bar area where the others already are waiting in silence. A few minutes later Tor walks in, his expression thunderous, but that is to be expected with one of his men missing. Then right behind him Zane and a woman walk in.

Zane's hair is pulled back into a ponytail, his blue eyes that are so much like Draco's, looking around until they clash with his brother's. The tension between the two is palpable. I notice Katrina sliding her hand into Draco's. The woman next to Zane stops, stepping to the side as Tor and Zane continue. Her hair is a shiny dark brown, her expression hard to read behind her sunglasses, and the hair falling forward to hide part of her face.

Her leather pants and jacket show that she is a rider, or at least a pillion that is used to being on a bike as her jacket has traces of long use. "Well, isn't this cosy? Everyone came out to welcome me," Zane states, his eyes still holding his brother's, his expression hard to read. '

Tor and Zane come to a stop in the centre of the room. The air charged with anger.

"Zane," Draco greets in a neutral tone.

"Hello, Brother," Zane greets sarcastically. "Looks like hell has just frozen over."

One day these two will have to find a common ground or agree to stay out of each other's way, because when they are both together, it's evident that there is resentment between the two, and only they know what it is.

"You are here to help find Tal so leave the past for now and do what you were asked to do," Draco orders in a low tone.

Zane lifts his hand and salutes him. "Of course, oh wise one!" he says sarcastically, which has Katrina lift her hand to Draco's chest when I see him take a step forward. I have always been impressed by the way Zane has no fear of Draco's wrath. If there is one person that will make any of us shake in our boots, it's Draco when he's in a rage.

"Violet!" Zane calls, which has all eyes move towards the woman that steps away from the wall where she was leaning, and towards Zane. "Violet is with me," he says, looking around. "She has a special gift that will help us find Tal."

At first, I thought that Violet was his mate, but she isn't, as their energy is not at peace with each other. She lifts her hand to her sunglasses, pulling them off, as she stands up straight looking at everyone. I hear a gasp from one of the women as they look into her eyes. There is no expression on her face as she faces all of us. Her eyes are such a light green that they seem completely white. "Who is going to take us to Tal's room so that we can get a trace on him?" Zane asks.

No one comes forward, so leaning down, I kiss Siena lightly on the lips. "Love you," I whisper, enjoying her little smile of pleasure just before stepping forward to take Zane and Violet to Tal's room. I have a feeling that this is the beginning of a long tempestuous time for the club, a time where we all need to be at peace with each other, and make certain that our mates are aware that they are part of this fight with us.

THE END.

A MESSAGE FROM ALEXI FERREIRA

Thank you so much for reading EIRIK and SIENA's book. This is book four in the Elemental's CT MC series. I hope you enjoyed your journey into the life of these bad boy alpha bikers and their women. **If you enjoyed this book, please consider leaving a review. Reviews help authors like me stay visible and help bring others to my series**. Next book in the Elemental's will be TAL (book 5).

ABOUT THE AUTHOR
Alexi Ferreira, loves the idea of Alpha Men who take charge

are possessive and care for their woman. She creates books that take you on an emotional journey whether tears, laughter or just steamy hotness. She loves to connect with readers and interacting with them through social media or even old fashioned email.

She currently lives in the United Kingdom. Books she has written are:

- Wulf (Book 1) Elemental's MC
- Bjarni (Book 2) Elemental's MC
- Brandr (Book 3) Elemental's MC
- Ceric (Book 4) Elemental's MC
- Bion (Book 5) Elemental's MC
- Cassius (Book 6) Elemental's MC
- Celmund (Book 7) Elemental's MC
- Burkhart (Book 8) Elemental's MC
- Caelius (Book 9) Elemental's MC
- Draco Salvation (Book 10) Elemental's MC
- Draco Wrath (Book 10) Elemental's MC

- Tormented (Book 1) Bratva Fury
- Turmoil (Book 2) Bratva Fury
- Mayhem (Book 3) Bratva Fury
- Fury (Book 4) Bratva Fury

Join her Social Media platforms to stay up to date as well as take part in giveaways and just let her know how you feel about her books!

Link: https://www.alexiferreira.writer.com/subscribe

WULF (Book 1) in the Elemental's MC series.

WULF

She is mine, they can try and get to her but they won't succeed, I will go through hell to protect her. No one touches what is mine. I will shake the earth itself, no one will be safe. My brothers and I are a family the club is my home but she is my soul the light to my darkness.

JAS

I have always felt like I didn't belong. Until I met Wulf. He takes me away from everything I know and introduces me to a life that I never expected. Now instead of being alone I have the whole mc as family, but I am in danger. Before everyone treated me as if I was a freak. But he understands me.

TORMENTED (book 1) Bratva Fury series.

JADE
I was minding my own business, simply working until Alexei the boss for the bratva mafia decided to take me. Having run away from a violent man before, I made a promise to myself this wouldn't happen again, but he doesn't give me a choice. I'm thrown into a world of violence, but this man of such vengeance almost hatred towards some can offer such love and safety when in his arms, something I have never experienced before.

ALEXEI
There's a war looming, hanging overhead like a dark cloud. This is the worst time to allow somebody into my life, but when I laid eyes on jade all logic and rational thought left me. I will protect her even if from herself, whoever comes for me is one thing, but to harm her will mean certain death, even if it kills me trying. She is my everything, my reason to live and if fate wants it, my reason to die.

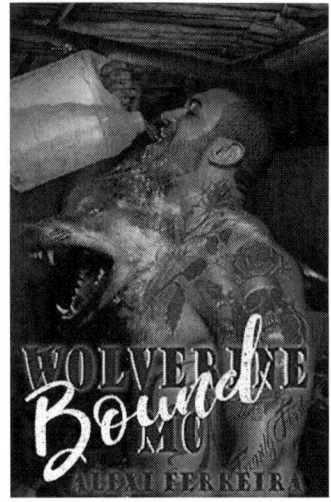

BOUND (book 1) Wolverine MC.

HUNTER
I have wondered if I would ever find my soulmate, the woman that would calm my soul. Now that I've found her she is mine, she just doesn't know it yet. Her ex thinks that he can stalk my woman and there will be no repercussions , well he has terrorized her enough. I will make sure that no one ever hurts her again. Anyone that tries to mess with her will have to deal with me and the whole WOLVERINE MC.

DAKOTA
This is a bad idea, but when I'm with hunter I feel safe, and wanted, something that I haven't felt in a long time. He has my heart racing with a single glance, there is a bond between us that I can't deny. Being part of an mc is intimidating, but they are protective and like family, I know it's a mistake but I have never felt more at home or complete as I do now.